HIS STORY

GOD'S PURPOSE AND PLAN
FROM GENESIS TO REVELATION

ADRIAN ROGERS

innovo
PUBLISHING
innovopublishing.com

Published by Innovo Publishing, LLC
www.innovopublishing.com
1-888-546-2111

Providing Full-Service Publishing Services for Christian Authors, Artists &
Ministries: Hardbacks, Paperbacks, eBooks, Audiobooks, Music, Screenplays,
& Courses

HIS STORY
God's Purpose and Plan from Genesis to Revelation

ISBN: 978-1-61314-581-4

Cover Design: Collin Houseal
Interior Layout: Innovo Publishing, LLC
Printed in the United States of America
U.S. Printing History
First Edition: 2020

CONTENTS

INTRODUCTION
... 7 ...

THE CREATION
... 9 ...

THE COVENANT
... 21 ...

THE CRADLE
... 37 ...

THE CUP
... 49 ...

THE CROWN
... 61 ...

THE CROSS
... 73 ...

THE CONQUEST
... 87 ...

THE COMING
... 99 ...

INTRODUCTION

S imple.
For most of us, we like things made very clear and simple. Complicated, convoluted, and multi-faceted explanations can leave us all scratching our heads. However, when someone can take an issue and explain it in a clear, plain, and straightforward manner, we are so thankful.

That's what this book is all about. Adrian Rogers has masterfully and simply taken the largest components of the Bible and broken them into eight sections.

As you read, you will learn about the pages of Scripture in these categories:

- The Creation
- The Covenant
- The Cradle
- The Cup
- The Crown
- The Cross
- The Conquest
- The Coming

Our hope is that you will read and begin to better understand the message of the Bible from start to finish. You'll start with the God of creation, learning about His power, His purpose, and His personal interest in your life. Then, you'll move to the wonderful covenant that God made with Abraham and his family.

Going forward, you will discover the cradle and the mystery, ministry, and majesty of Jesus' birth. From there, you will read about the cup that our Savior bore as you learn about the contents of the cup, the communion of the cup, and the consumption of the cup. After the cup, you will read about Jesus' crown of thorns—its mystery, misery, mockery, ministry, and majesty.

As you continue on, you will peruse pages leading you to the cross of Christ. In this section, you will gain insights on the sufferings of the cross, the satisfaction of the cross, and the salvation of the cross. Further, you will read about the conquest of Jesus; His preaching convinces, His persecution continues, His power confronts, His presence compels, and His people confess.

The final chapter will share the future hope of His coming. Jesus is coming again! He is coming visibly, victoriously, and vengefully. We should look forward to His coming!

Ultimately, the Bible is all about the Lord Jesus. We pray that you will find Him, enjoy Him, and get to know Him more as you read through *His Story: God's Purpose and Plan from Genesis to Revelation.*

Chapter 1

THE CREATION

"In the beginning God created the heavens and the earth" (Genesis 1:1). I believe this verse has been read more than any other piece of literature in all of history. How many people have started out to read the Bible through, and never did? But they got as far as Genesis 1:1.

It is a wonderful verse, and we will never begin to exhaust it with our little teacup minds and this great ocean of truth that is found in Genesis 1:1. But you must understand at least part of it, and you must believe all of it, because it is foundational. You'll never really comprehend anything else in the Bible unless you understand Genesis 1:1, "In the beginning God created the heavens and the earth." This is foundational truth; functional truth—you must believe it. The key to the rest of the Bible is hung right here by the front door.

The God Who is Presented

The first thing I want you to see about the God of all creation is that He is the God who is presented. Why did I choose that word, *presented?* Because the fact of God is not argued here, and the nature and being of God are not explained. He is just presented. No philosophy, no argument, no apology, no explanation; just "In the beginning God..." The Bible writers never tried to explain the existence of God; nor should you. You are very foolish if you try to prove God. People talk about the proofs for God, but there are none. Don't let that shock you! The finite can never prove the infinite, you see. The Bible writers *presented* God. God doesn't need any proof, and you are incapable of proving God! "Can you search out the deep things of God? Can you find out the limits of the Almighty?" (Job 11:7). Sometimes an atheist will swagger up to a believer and say, "Prove there is a God." That never threatens me—I just smile and say, "Prove there is *no* God."

The finite mind can never prove or disprove the infinite God. He does not lie in the realm of proof. To try to prove God by looking through physical, material things would be like tearing a piano apart to find the *Hallelujah Chorus*. You don't prove God, and you don't disprove God—you believe in God. Sometimes that is leveled against us Christians as though it is an accusation. *"You just accept by faith that there's a God."* That's right! And let me tell you what the unbeliever does: he accepts, *by faith*, that there is no God! He has never proven there is no God. All men are believers—I choose to believe in God; the atheist chooses not to believe in God.

An atheist is not an unbeliever because he has intellectual superiority. Some of the finest minds this world has ever known have been given to the gospel of Christ. You show me a brilliant man who does not believe in God; I will show you a brilliant man who does. You show me a stupid man who doesn't believe in God, and I'll show you some stupid people who do.

It is not a matter of intellect, and it is not a matter of reason. Not that these things are unreasonable; they are *above* reason. He is the God who is presented, not the God who is argued. If a man does not believe in God, it's because he doesn't want to believe in God. There is no explanation of God given in the Bible, no philosophy for God. God is just presented: "In the beginning God." And, there's not much said about atheism in the Bible. As far as I can see, one-half of one verse deals with atheism: Psalm 53:1a says," The fool has said in his heart, 'There is no God.'" That's it, and then God goes on to another subject.

This word, *fool*, is the word *nabal* in Hebrew. It doesn't refer to a man who has unfurnished rooms to rent upstairs, lacking intellectually. The word *nabal* here means a *morally perverse* person.

Notice what it says. "The fool has said in his heart, 'There is no God.'" The problem with the man who doesn't believe in God is in his heart, not his head. It is not that he *cannot* believe—it is that he *will not* believe. He doesn't wish to believe. And this verse in Psalm 53 literally translates as, "The fool has said in his heart, 'No God.'" What is the difference between "there is no God" and "no God"?

For example, after the holidays, many of us have determined to lose a few pounds. So, when somebody serves you a meal and says, "Would you like some pie?" I say, "No pie." That doesn't mean there is no pie. I just mean, "No pie for me. I don't want any."

This is literally what the fool is saying. "The fool has said in his heart, 'No God.'" That is, "I don't want any, thank you." In his heart of hearts, he knows better. Evolution and atheism and all of that exists as a bias against God, not because a man has reasonably and logically figured it out.

Do you know what the atheist believes? Nothing times nobody equals everything. That's not logical, is it? Of course not. You see, it's not that he's figured it out. It's not that he is forced upon that belief by logic. *He does not want the idea of God.* "The fool has said in his heart, 'No God.'" God is not argued in the Bible. The reason people don't believe in God is found in Romans 1:28, "And even as they did not like to retain God in *their* knowledge, God gave them over to a debased mind, to do those things which are not fitting." The idea of God gives them an uneasy feeling, so they think that if they can get rid of the idea of God, they can get rid of that uneasy feeling.

But a man never gets rid of the uneasy feeling of not having God in his heart. He is like a man who bought a new boomerang, and killed himself trying to throw the old one away. It just keeps coming back, and coming back, and coming back. The fool has said in his heart, "There is no God..." (Psalm 53:1a). They don't like to retain the knowledge of God in their mind, but you find in Genesis 1:1 that He is, firstly, the God who is presented. Not argued, philosophized, explained, or apologized for; just, "Here it is, folks."

The God Who is Powerful

The second thing to notice is that He is the God who is powerful. Genesis 1:1 says, "In the beginning God *created* the heavens and the earth." He is the God of all creation. Therefore, He is the God of all power. And the word *created* here is the Hebrew word *bara*. It is used about fifty times in the Bible, and it always speaks of something that only God can do; that is, to make something out of nothing.

Hebrews 11:3 puts it this way, "By faith we understand that the worlds were framed by the word of God, so that the things which are seen were not made of things which are visible." Anything you make, you make out of something else. Right? But the things that we see were not made out of things which do appear. The only way you will understand that is by faith. By faith, we understand that by the word of God the worlds were framed. God spoke and it was so. *Ex nihilo*—out of nothing—God made it all. And that speaks of the mighty power of God.

I like what another preacher had to say about it. He said, "God stepped from behind the curtain of nowhere, stood of the platform of nothing, and spoke a universe into existence." "In the beginning God created the heavens and the earth" (Genesis 1:1). And as we look at His creation, how amazed we ought to be.

There are an estimated 30 trillion cells in the human body. But you see, the cell, small as it is, is not the smallest unit. Smaller than that is the atom. And the atom is mostly empty space. We think we are hard substance, but if you were to take the nothingness out of everybody, from more than 4 billion people on this globe, and squeeze the emptiness out of them, you could put us all—4 billion-plus people—in a gallon pail. We're mostly nothing.

Light travels at 186,282 miles per second. If you were to catch a light beam and start traveling, you'd be at the moon in two seconds. In four years, you'd be at the nearest star. But, friend, even traveling at 186,282 miles per second, you would go more than 10 billion years before you reached the edge of the known universe—and who knows what's beyond that. The vastness of this mighty universe! God spoke and it was so. And God made it all out of nothing.

Now, when I say there are no *proofs* for God, I don't mean there are no *evidences* for God. Do you understand the difference between proof and evidence? If you see a watch, then you say there must be a watchmaker, right? What about the atomic clock of the universe? Do you think that just happened? Scientists don't create scientific laws; they discover them. They are no more able to create them than Columbus was able to create North America—he discovered it.

If there is a city water system, there must be an engineer who designed it. What about the hydraulic cycle in the atmosphere, God's processes of hydrology? We look at beautiful buildings and we see design and purpose. We say there must be an architect. Well, what about the human body? "I will praise You, for I am fearfully *and* wonderfully made…" says Psalm 139:14a. As we look around, everywhere we see that He is a God of might and miracle and power. He is a God of power, and we see it in Genesis 1:1. The evolutionist believes it all just happened, that billions of years will turn frogs into princes.

Know the difference between *making* something and *creating* something. People can make things: when you make something, you take a simple form and put it into a more complex form. My wife can make biscuits, but she doesn't create them. She does it with creativity! But she does not create biscuits. She takes already-existing materials and puts them together, and therefore she makes biscuits. You see, to *create*, you have to make something out of nothing—and only God can do that.

I once saw in the newspapers, "Scientists Create Life in Laboratory." Let me tell you something, no scientist ever created anything. He can't do that until he starts making something out of nothing! Suppose your father is a master builder of fine homes, and you watch your father studiously to see what He has done. And then, in your father's absence, you take your father's building plans, tools, and materials, and you build a chicken coop. When you finish, you stand back, stick out your puny chest, and say, "You see that chicken coop? That proves my father doesn't exist."

That is what men do when they come into the laboratory and take God's materials, God's tools, and God's methods and make some life-*like* substances—which is not *life*, in the true form of the word. A rearrangement, by genetic engineering, of that which God has already brought into existence *is not creation*. That is *making* something—in many instances, it is *distorting* something. I am fearfully afraid of what mankind is able to do and what mankind will do with his so-called vaunted knowledge and wisdom. But only God has the power to create.

The God Who is Purposeful

The third thing about this great God is that He is the God who is purposeful. "In the beginning God created the heavens and the earth" (Genesis 1:1). He made it all. Why? He had a reason, a purpose for doing it. And we don't have to guess at the purpose. I want to give you three reasons why God made it all. What was His purpose?

They were created for His pleasure.

Revelation 4:11, "You are worthy, O Lord, To receive glory and honor and power; For You created all things, And by Your will they exist and were created." God made it because He wanted to, and He didn't have to get your opinion or permission. As He said to Job, "Where were you when I laid the foundations of the earth? Tell *Me*, if you have understanding" (Job 38:4). He is a sovereign God, and it was created for His pleasure.

They were created for His praise.

"For of Him and through Him and to Him *are* all things, to whom *be* glory forever. Amen" (Romans 11:36). What does that mean? The same thing Psalm 150:6 means when it says, "Let everything that has breath praise the LORD. Praise the LORD!"

Everything that is created is created to bring glory to Him. Therefore, the trees lift their leafy arms and say, "Praise God!" The beautiful flowers and the birds on the wing say, "Praise God!" The mighty oceans heave their billows. Niagara rolls and rolls and says, "Praise God!" God made a fish to swim in the sea, a bird to sail through the air. But if you take that bird out of the air and put him in the sea, he's an unhappy bird. Take that fish out of the sea and put him in the tree, and, to say the least, he's not doing what he was meant to do.

It is "for in Him we live and move and have our being..." (see Acts 17:28), and until you learn to praise God you'll never learn the meaning of life. You were created to praise Him. "Let everything that has breath praise the LORD. Praise the LORD!"

They were created for His people.

After God created these things, He stepped back and said, "That's good." You can see that throughout Genesis 1. He saw that man didn't have a wife, And the LORD God said, "*It is* not good that man should be alone; I will make him a helper comparable to him" (Genesis 2:18). These verses tell us it is God's plan that man's good be effected. You see, when God created everything, He had in mind His supreme creation, which is man. And so He made it not only for His pleasure and His praise, but for His people. In a very real sense of the word, He gave it to us, and He told us to have dominion and enjoy it.

Now I want to tell you what the devil wants to do. The devil wants to get you thinking negatively about God; thinking that God is not a good God. And with all of the unction, function, and emotion of my soul I pray that God will etch this into your consciousness: *God is a good God.* God made it for His glory, and for your good; for His praise, but for His people.

I want to give you three verses. Keep these in your mind and live by them, because they will help you. Sin *begins* with thinking negatively about God, and sin *causes* us to think negatively about God.

- "Delight yourself also in the Lord, And He shall give you the desires of your heart" (Psalm 37:4).
- "For the Lord God is a sun and shield; The Lord will give grace and glory; no good thing will He withhold from those who walk uprightly" (Psalm 84:11). Did you hear that? "No good thing." If it will make you healthy, happy, holy, and wholesome, God says, "Help yourself. I love you; I made it for you." God wants for you what you'd want for yourself if you had enough sense to want it! God is such a good God.

- "Command those who are rich in this present age not to be haughty, nor to trust in uncertain riches but in the living God, who gives us richly all things to enjoy" (1 Timothy 6:17). It speaks of God "who gives us richly all things to enjoy." God wants you to enjoy these flowers. God wants you to enjoy the fish and the fowl. Sometimes we think that because we're Christians, we can't enjoy these things. Don't ever think that God's physical, material universe is evil! When God made it, God said, "It is good." The same God that made the pork made the strawberries.

God is such a good God, a wonderful God, a glorious God. He is a God who is presented and powerful, but also a God who is purposeful. God had a purpose in all of this creation: for His pleasure, for His praise, for His people. God flung out the stars and scooped out the seas and heaped up the mountains, and God spoke it and it stood fast.

The God Who is Personal

Now for the fourth thing to see about the nature of God. Not only is He the God who is presented, powerful, and purposeful, but He is the God who is personal.

What do we mean by personal? That He is a person! I don't mean that He has eyes, ears, hands, and feet. When the Bible uses those images of God, it is using language that the theologians call "anthropomorphic language." That is, speaking of God as if He had those physical abilities and characteristics, so that we can understand when the Bible speaks of the eyes of the Lord and the hands of the Lord. God is a spirit, but He is a person.

What do we mean by a person? That God has the characteristics of personhood: intelligence, emotion, and will. God is a person, not an impersonal being. "In the beginning God created the heavens and the earth" literally translates as, "In the beginning *Elohim* created the heavens and the earth." That is the Hebrew word for God: *Elohim*. *El*, which speaks that He is God of might. *El* means strength and unlimited power.

Actually, *Elohim* is a plural noun. It seems to say, "In the beginning *Gods...*"; although it doesn't, for there is only one God. But look in Genesis 1:26a, and it says, Then God [singular, this time] said, "Let Us make man in Our image, according to Our likeness..." (words in brackets added). Is that just poor grammar? That time it is singular, but there is that plural noun: God, *Elohim*. I believe right here on the threshold of the Bible we see an indication of the nature of God as shown in the Holy Trinity: God the Father, God the Son, and God the Holy Spirit, because as you study the Bible, you find out that all three were present at Creation. All three were active there. Was it *Jehovah* God who created the world? *Elohim* God who created the world? Or was it the Lord *Jesus* who created the world, for the Bible says in the New Testament that Jesus did it all. "All things were made through Him, and without Him nothing was made that was made" (John 1:3). There is no contradiction there. You find it all in this little triune noun, this plural noun here: *Elohim*.

Aren't you glad we find the Savior, and the Holy Spirit, *and* the Father in chapter 1, verse 1 of the Word of God? In the beginning, Elohim—the God with whom nothing is impossible, who always keeps His word; the triune God: Father, Son, and Holy Spirit—created—for His pleasure, His praise, and His people—the heavens and the earth.

Think of all the theological errors that are being refuted here. Atheism is refuted; this verse speaks of God. Polytheism is refuted; it speaks of *one* God. Pantheism, which says that God and nature are the same, is refuted; God is shown here not as a part of nature, but as creating nature. Materialism, the belief in the eternality of matter and material, is refuted. All of these errors are set aside as we see this one, great, personal God. "In the beginning God created the heavens and the earth" (Genesis 1:1).

He is a real God and a revealed God. Now, I said you could never prove God, but that doesn't mean that you can never *know* God. You do not know God by proving God; you know God by revelation. In Romans 1, the Bible speaks of people who don't have a leg to stand on, and are without excuse. They claim to be atheists, but God doesn't buy it. And here's why: God says they are without excuse because everybody has an innate awareness of God.

Because what may be known of God is manifest in them, for God has shown it to them. For since the creation of the world His invisible attributes are clearly seen, being understood by the things that are made, even His eternal power and Godhead, so that they are without excuse. (Romans 1:19-20)

"Because what may be known of God is manifest in them…"—that is the inner awareness. "For God has shown it to them…"—there is the outer, objective evidence. "For since the creation of the world His invisible attributes are clearly seen, being understood by the things that are made…"—that is, you can clearly see from a creation that there is a creator. "Even his eternal power;"—for He is a God of power and a God of purpose, "so that they are without excuse."

You will never come to the Judgment and say, "God, I want to be excused. I had intellectual difficulties."

God will say, "You were a sinner. The fool has said in his heart, 'no God.'" There is no excuse for not believing in God.

No one is a natural-born atheist. Someone has to come along with a convoluted argument to make an atheist out of you. I heard about a child who was raised in atheistic family; one day, the child said to his mother and daddy, "Do you think God knows we don't believe in Him?"

We are, by nature, believers in God, "for God has shown it to them." It is in us. We know, not by reason, but by revelation. I'm not saying you have to crucify your intellect, but I am saying that when you get right down to it, God has "hidden these things from the wise and the prudent and revealed them to babes" (see Luke 10:21). He is a personal God, and because He is not just some blind force, God has chosen to reveal Himself to you and make Himself known. The inner awareness, the outer objectivity in nature, the revelation of the Bible, and primarily Jesus Christ, have revealed the Father to us. He is a real person. He is a revealed person.

If these things are true about God (and they are) and if you believe Genesis 1:1 (I trust that you do), that "In the beginning God created the heavens and the earth," then there are at least two conclusions that are forced upon you. There are many others, but these two I want to bring to your mind and your heart, as God the Holy Spirit helps me.

You have a moral responsibility to God.

Do you know what Ecclesiastes 12:1a says? "Remember now your Creator in the days of your youth..." And Isaiah 45:9a, "Woe to him who strives with his Maker!" If God made you, you have an obligation to Him.

Not only did God create you, but God redeemed you. God bought you with His blood. I guess every preacher has told the story of the little fellow who lost his little red sailboat that he had made. It sailed away from him across the pond. Later on, he saw it in a second-hand store and the proprietor made him buy it back! He bought it back, and he carried that little sailboat out of that second-hand store and hugged it to his chest, and he said, "Little sailboat, you're mine—you're twice mine. You're mine because I made you, and mine because I bought you back."

I think that God would say that to us. "Christian, you're mine. You are twice mine. Mine because I created you, and Mine because I redeemed you. You are not your own, 'For you were bought at a price; therefore glorify God in your body and in your spirit, which are God's'" (1 Corinthians 6:20). If you believe Genesis 1:1, you have to believe we have a moral responsibility to God. If we don't meet it, we'll answer for it at the Judgment.

God has an obligation to us.

Not only do we have an obligation, a moral responsibility, to God, but do you know that God has an obligation to us? Now, I mean to speak reverently when I talk about God having an obligation to anybody. But when God made us, He obligated Himself to us. When we bring children into the world, aren't we obligated to those children? Indeed we are. There is a responsibility that comes with bringing children into the world. And there was a responsibility that was incumbent upon God when God created us, and God made Himself responsible to us. The Bible speaks of God in 1 Peter 4:19 as a faithful Creator. He wouldn't just make this world, wind it up, and fling it out into space and turn His back on it. No! He made it; He must look after it. Isaiah 43:1-3 says,

But now, thus says the LORD, who created you, O Jacob, And He who formed you, O Israel: "Fear not, for I have redeemed you; I have called you by your name; You are Mine. When you pass through the waters, I will be with you; And through the rivers, they shall not overflow you. When you walk through the fire, you shall not be burned, Nor shall the flame scorch you. For I am the LORD your God, The Holy One of Israel, your Savior; I gave Egypt for your ransom, Ethiopia and Seba in your place."

God is saying, "I made you, I saved you, I'm going to take care of you." Friend, He will. This God who is a God of power, who is a personal God and a purposeful God, made you for a purpose. He is going to watch over you and take care of you.

When God created this first world, He stepped back and said, "It is finished!" and then He rested. But sin came in and marred His first creation, so God set about to make a new creation. Do you know what the new creation is? The Church. And when Jesus Christ died on the cross, when that last drop of blood hit the ground below, Jesus said, "It is finished!" (John 19:30). What was finished? A new creation. "Therefore, if anyone *is* in Christ, *he is* a new creation…" (2 Corinthians 5:17a). Even when sin marred God's original creation, God didn't say, "I'm finished with it." God made it and God stayed with it. We have an obligation to God; indeed we do. And correspondingly, God has an obligation to us. Isn't that a wonderful arrangement? I like it.

It took a miracle to put the stars in place;
It took a miracle to hang the world in space.
But when He saved my soul,
Cleansed and made me whole,
It took a miracle of love and grace!

(From the song *"It Took a Miracle"*; by John W. Peterson, 1948)

Chapter 2

THE COVENANT

L et's look at Genesis 17, beginning with verse 1.

> When Abram was ninety-nine years old, the LORD
> appeared to Abram and said to him, "I am Almighty
> God; walk before Me and be blameless. And I will make
> My covenant between Me and you, and will multiply
> you exceedingly. "Then Abram fell on his face, and
> God talked with him, saying: "As for Me, behold, My
> covenant is with you, and you shall be a father of many
> nations. No longer shall your name be called Abram,
> but your name shall be Abraham; for I have made you a
> father of many nations. (Genesis 17:1-5)

God added another Hebrew letter to the name of Abram. It
is the fifth letter in the Hebrew alphabet, and that letter is also the
word for *Spirit, breath,* or *wind* in the Old Testament. What God is
saying to Abram is, "I am putting My Spirit upon you." And the fact
that it was the *fifth* Hebrew letter reminds us that 5 is the number
of grace.

> No longer shall your name be called Abram, but your
> name shall be Abraham; for I have made you a father
> of many nations. I will make you exceedingly fruitful;

and I will make nations of you, and kings shall come from you. And I will establish My covenant between Me and you and your descendants after you in their generations, for an everlasting covenant, to be God to you and your descendants after you. Also I give to you and your descendants after you the land in which you are a stranger, all the land of Canaan, as an everlasting possession; and I will be their God. (Genesis 17:5-8)

This is one of the most important documents ever written— far more important than the Declaration of Independence, the Mayflower Compact, or the Constitution of the United States of America. If you understand what God is saying here, you will be able to understand the history of the world, for what God is saying marks in color all of subsequent history.

This is an iron fist upon history to say that certain things are going to be done. It is God's plan to bless you, and me, and the nations of the world. This is a blessing, a promise that has changed the world, and it will help us understand what is happening in this age.

The Covenant Plan

The Covenant Promise

Notice the covenant promise in the first three verses of Genesis 17. In verse 2, it says that God is going to make a covenant between God and Abraham. It is an unbreakable, unchangeable, immutable covenant. It is a promise that will last unconditionally. Sometimes, God makes promises that are conditional promises. That is, God says, "If you'll do this, I'll do that. If you don't do this, I won't do that." But this is an *unconditional* covenant promise.

The Covenant Principle

This is a covenant promise based on the covenant principle of *grace*. It is not due to anything inherent in Abraham, and not based on anything that Abraham has done or will do. As a matter of fact,

God is doing all of the talking. Abraham is on his face, listening, as God makes a covenant with him.

The Covenant People

In Genesis 17:7, God says, "And I will establish My covenant between Me and you and your descendants after you...." What seed is He talking about? God is talking about the Hebrews, the Jewish race. In Genesis 17:21, God continues: "But My covenant I will establish with Isaac, whom Sarah shall bear to you at this set time next year." God is not talking about Ishmael, who is the progenitor of the Arab race. He is talking about Isaac, the progenitor of the Jews. The people that this covenant primarily concerns are the Jewish people, the descendants—the seed—of Abraham. And also, God is talking here about Abraham's greatest son, the Lord Jesus Christ, who in the fullest sense is the seed of Abraham.

The Covenant Period

Notice in Genesis 17:7 that it shall be "an everlasting covenant." That is, it will never grow old, never wear out, never be changed. It is an everlasting, and therefore an irrevocable and unchangeable, covenant. It will last through the eons of the ages.

The Covenant Place

Not only does the covenant involve a people, but also a covenant place. "Also I give to you and your descendants after you the land in which you are a stranger, all the land of Canaan, as an everlasting possession; and I will be their God" (Genesis 17:8).

God said, "I'm going to give this land, the Middle East," that is, Palestine, the Holy Land, Israel. "I will give it to you, Abraham, and to your descendants through Isaac for an everlasting possession."

The eyes of the world are upon that tiny state of Israel, and that's the way it should be, because the Jews are the people of destiny. As the Jew goes, so goes the world. The Jew is God's yardstick, God's blueprint, God's measuring rod, God's program for what He is going to do with the other nations of the world.

And the Jews and the land are wrapped up together. So not only do we need to keep our eyes upon the people, but we need to keep our eyes upon the place of those people.

I'm talking about the real estate which in Genesis 17:8 God calls "the land of Canaan," that He gave to Abraham and to Abraham's descendants. I want you to see how it is the very center of the earth. "Thus says the Lord GOD: 'This is Jerusalem; I have set her in the midst of the nations and the countries all around her'" (Ezekiel 5:5).

The Geographical Center

This seemingly insignificant little parcel of ground is the hub of three mighty continents—Africa, Asia, and Europe. It is an ancient military and economic crossroads, and some have called it "the navel of the earth." It is the geographical center of the earth. And in the Bible, when directions are given, they are "north of Israel", or "south of Israel". That is God's plan, for it to be the geographical center.

The Revelation Center

It was from Canaan that Moses wrote. It was from Canaan that the prophets spoke. It was from Canaan that we received the Bible.

The Spiritual Center

It was in Canaan that Jesus Christ was born. It was there that Jesus Christ lived and walked and taught. He never left until He left to go to heaven. It is there that Jesus died, was buried, rose, and it is to the land of Canaan that Jesus Christ will come again.

The Prophetic Center

This land of Palestine, Egypt, Canaan, is the only place and the only people whose prophecy was minutely foretold centuries before it came to pass.

The Storm Center

We are seeing the nations of the world line up around this little nation of Israel. The clouds are gathering, and I believe we are seeing, even in our day, the foregleams of the Battle of Armageddon, which will be fought in Canaan (see Revelation 16). It is the storm center of the entire world.

The Peace Center

But it is also the peace center of the world. One of these days, the lamb and the lion will lie down together, and the earth will be filled with the knowledge of the glory of the Lord, as waters that cover the sea. The desert will blossom as a rose. Jesus will reign for a thousand years from this place, Canaan, and there will be peace upon this earth.

That is the reason the Bible tells us to pray for the peace of Jerusalem. There will never be peace on earth until there is peace in Jerusalem, and there will never be peace in Jerusalem until Jesus Christ rules and reigns there. When you are praying for the peace of Jerusalem, you are also praying for the Prince of Peace, the Lord Jesus Christ, to come again.

The Glory Center

And it will be the glory center of the world as Jesus, the Lord, Savior, and Messiah will rule and reign from the throne of His father David. Jesus is the true seed of Abraham, one who came from the loins of Abraham, one who came from the loins of David, and one who will sit upon the throne of His father David and dispense the covenant blessings of Abraham. How grateful we are for what God is doing in keeping His promise to Abraham so long ago.

The Covenant Picture

Now it came to pass after these things that God tested Abraham, and said to him, "Abraham!" And he said, "Here I am." Then He said, "Take now your son, your only son Isaac, whom you love, and go to the land of Moriah, and offer him there as a burnt offering on one of the mountains of which I shall tell you. (Genesis 22:1-2)

When Abraham and Isaac in the Old Testament went up Mount Moriah for a very special offering, it was a dress rehearsal for Calvary. It was a picture, a prophecy, an Old Testament portrait of the death, burial, and resurrection of Jesus Christ.

Abraham lived centuries before Jesus Christ was born in flesh upon this earth, but the Lord Jesus said in John 8:56, "Your father Abraham rejoiced to see My day, and he saw it and was glad." Galatians 3:8, "And the Scripture, foreseeing that God would justify the Gentiles by faith, preached the gospel to Abraham beforehand, saying, "In you all the nations shall be blessed." And so we read that the Gospel was preached to Abraham.

A Special Person

The first thing I want you to see in Genesis 22 is a special person—Isaac. Isaac, the son of Abraham, was a picture of the Lord Jesus Christ, and let me tell you how:

His birth was prophesied. Turn back to Genesis 18, where the LORD has come to Abraham and Abraham is entertaining the LORD and two angels.

Then they said to him, "Where is Sarah your wife?" So he said, "Here, in the tent." And He said, "I will certainly return to you according to the time of life, and behold, Sarah your wife shall have a son." (Sarah was listening in the tent door which was behind him.) Now Abraham and Sarah were old, well advanced in age; and Sarah had passed the age of childbearing. Therefore Sarah laughed within herself, saying, "After I have grown old, shall I have pleasure, my lord being old also?" And the LORD said to Abraham, "Why did Sarah laugh, saying, 'Shall I surely bear a child, since I am old?' Is anything too hard for the LORD? At the appointed time I will return to you, according to the time of life, and Sarah shall have a son." (Genesis 18:9-14)

Here a birth is prophesied, and it is a miracle birth. Isaac was born of a miracle, just as the Lord Jesus was born of a miracle in His virgin birth.

His birthdate was preset. God said to Sarah and Abraham that He would do it "at the appointed time." Ephesians 1:10 tells us that the Lord Jesus Christ came into this world "...in the dispensation of the fullness of the times...."

This child Isaac was named before he was born. Look in Genesis 17:19a, "Then God said: 'No, Sarah your wife shall bear you a son, and you shall call his name Isaac....'" Jesus was named before He was born: Matthew 1:21a, "And she will bring forth a Son, and you shall call His name JESUS...."

Isaac was conceived by a miracle, just as Jesus was conceived by a miracle. Isaiah 7:14, "Therefore the Lord Himself will give you a sign: Behold, the virgin shall conceive and bear a Son, and shall call His name Immanuel." When Sarah and Abraham came together and had a son; that was a miracle. When little Isaac was born, Abraham was 100 years old and Sarah was 90. I can see Abraham coming out of the maternity ward on a cane, saying, "It's a boy!"

The birth of Isaac was prophesied. He came at a set time; his name was given before he was born. His birth was because of a miracle conception. And he was counted as Abraham's only beloved son.

> Now it came to pass after these things that God tested Abraham, and said to him, "Abraham!" And he said, "Here I am." Then He said, "Take now your son, your only son Isaac, whom you love, and go to the land of Moriah, and offer him there as a burnt offering on one of the mountains of which I shall tell you." (Genesis 22:1-2)

God tested Abraham. "Take now your son, your only son Isaac, whom you love..." Now what does that remind you of? John 3:16, "For God so loved the world that He gave His only begotten

Son, that whoever believes in Him should not perish but have everlasting life."

Here was this boy Isaac, conceived by a miracle, counted as Abraham's only son, and now God the Father says, "Abraham, I want you to offer your only son as a burnt offering." And Abraham saw his son raised from the dead. Now, he did not see him *literally* raised from the dead, but he saw him *figuratively* raised from the dead.

Genesis 22:4 states, "Then on the third day Abraham lifted his eyes and saw the place afar off." That is, he saw Mount Moriah. From the time God told Abraham to put his son to death till the time they saw Mount Moriah was three days, just as the Lord Jesus Christ was in the grave three days and three nights. In the heart and mind of Abraham, Isaac was as good as dead for three days.

You might say, "*Pastor, you're pushing the point here.*" No, I'm not. The Bible says in Hebrews 11:19 that Abraham did this, and "Concluding that God was able to raise him up, even from the dead, from which he also received him in a figurative sense." In a "figure," symbolically, Abraham received Isaac raised from the dead.

Can you see how Isaac pictures Jesus? Isaac was the son of prophecy and promise, his birth was at a set time, his name was given before he was born, and he was conceived of a miracle. He was the only beloved son, was offered up as a sacrifice, and was received from the dead. God has put an Old Testament Calvary here just to show us that Calvary was not incidental or accidental, that Calvary had been in the heart and mind of God before God created the universe.

A Specific Place

God didn't say "just any place." No—a *particular* place. Look again in Genesis 22:2,

> Then He [God] said, "Take now your son, your only son Isaac, whom you love, and go to the land of Moriah, and offer him there as a burnt offering on one of the mountains of which I shall tell you..." (Word in brackets added for clarity.)

And then, in verse 4, "Then on the third day Abraham lifted his eyes and saw the place afar off." What was the place? It was Mount Moriah, and *Moriah* means "foreseen of the Lord." Keep that in mind: here was a particular place in the heart and mind of God.

Of this magnificent globe called Planet Earth, God rejected many beautiful, magnificent places, and He took a little land there on the edge of the Mediterranean and calls it His land. That is the land of Israel. And then in the land of Israel, from Dan to Beersheba, God took one city and calls it *Jerusalem*, the city of the great king, the holy city. "The earth *is* the LORD's, and all its fullness, The world and those who dwell therein" (Psalm 24:1). God kept tightening the focus, and took one mountain from in that city, in that land, on that earth, in that solar system, in that galaxy. God calls that mountain, "My holy hill." What was so important about that?

Do you know where Moriah is? Mt. Moriah is Calvary. That is where the Temple was built—on Moriah. That is where Jesus died—on Moriah. And God said, "Now Abraham, take your son, your beloved son of miracle birth, whom I named, and whom I gave to you. Take that son to the place I will show you and sacrifice him there." A special person, a specific place. Doesn't it remind you of Luke 23:33? "And when they had come to the place called Calvary, there they crucified Him...."

A Solemn Purpose

Now Abraham and Isaac started going up Mount Moriah. The others who were with them could not go. "And Abraham said to his young men, 'Stay here with the donkey; the lad and I will go yonder and worship, and we will come back to you'" (Genesis 22:5). God the Father and God the Son have gone places you and I will never know. This is a picture of dark Gethsemane, when the Lord Jesus was alone with the Father (see Mark 14:32-41).

Can you imagine what must have gone through the heart and mind of Isaac? Can you imagine his suffering? Isaac looked at his father, and his father had fire. There were no matches in that day, so he had to carry a torch with him. This was going to be a burnt offering. Abraham had a fire in one hand, and a knife in the other.

As they are going up Mount Moriah, Isaac doesn't know what is about to transpire. He can tell there is a troubled look on his father's face,

> But Isaac spoke to Abraham his father and said, "My father!" And he said, "Here I am, my son." Then he said, "Look, the fire and the wood, but where is the lamb for a burnt offering?" And Abraham said, "My son, God will provide for Himself the lamb for a burnt offering." So the two of them went together. (Genesis 22:7-8)

Isaac is now beginning to understand that *he* is going to be the sacrifice.

> Then they came to the place of which God had told him. And Abraham built an altar there and placed the wood in order; and he bound Isaac his son and laid him on the altar, upon the wood. (Genesis 22:9)

Now don't get the idea here Isaac is a little baby boy. Isaac is a strapping teenage boy. Abraham is now well over a hundred years of age. Isaac could have outrun Abraham, or wrestled him to the ground and overpowered him. But Isaac allows himself to be bound. As the Savior said in Gethsemane, "nevertheless not My will, but Yours, be done." (Luke 22:42b) Isaac did not refuse to be a sacrifice, just like Jesus did not refuse when He laid down *His* life. People said, concerning Jesus, "He saved others; Himself He cannot save...." (Matthew 27:42a) It was Himself He *would* not save.

Look back at Genesis 22:6, "So Abraham took the wood of the burnt offering and laid *it* on Isaac his son; and he took the fire in his hand, and a knife, and the two of them went together." Here is Isaac carrying, as it were, the wood of his cross up Calvary.

Jesus laid aside the gold of His glory. He took the wood of our wickedness and the wood of our weakness. Doesn't this remind you of John 19:17? Speaking of Jesus, "And He, bearing His cross, went out to a place called *the Place* of a Skull, which is called in Hebrew, Golgotha" (John 19:17).

In Genesis 22:9-10,

Then they came to the place of which God had told him. And Abraham built an altar there and placed the wood in order; and he bound Isaac his son and laid him on the altar, upon the wood. And Abraham stretched out his hand and took the knife to slay his son.

The cord speaks of the binding power of sin. The knife speaks of the bleeding power of sin. The wood speaks of the burning power of sin. They speak of all that Jesus would suffer on that cross, for us. And they foretell a time when God would lay His own dear Son upon a cross and raise the knife of His fierce wrath against sin. You cannot imagine what it must have been like for Abraham at that moment. Don't think only about Isaac; thank God for Isaac, but think about Abraham also, who had to sacrifice his own son.

A Sacred Promise

Abraham is about to plunge that knife into the beating breast of his own dear son. But look—

But the Angel of the LORD called to him from heaven and said, "Abraham, Abraham!" So he said, "Here I am." And He said, "Do not lay your hand on the lad, or do anything to him; for now I know that you fear God, since you have not withheld your son, your only son, from Me." Then Abraham lifted his eyes and looked, and there behind him was a ram caught in a thicket by its horns. So Abraham went and took the ram, and offered it up for a burnt offering instead of his son. And Abraham called the name of the place, The-LORD-Will-Provide; as it is said to this day, "In the Mount of the LORD it shall be provided. (Genesis 22:11-14)

That knife did not fall upon Isaac, because one day it would fall upon Jesus. No longer is Isaac a picture of the Savior. God dramatically shifts the scene, and Isaac becomes a picture of me, and of *you*. He is there, destined to receive the knife, but there is a change.

God says, "Isaac, get up. There is a substitute for you." Abraham looks up, and there is a ram caught by its horns in a thicket. Its head is caught in thorns. Do you know what that was? It was a lamb crowned with thorns! (See Matthew 27:29) And God says, "Take this one! Sacrifice him instead of Isaac." Isaac is up, and a substitute is down. What a picture of Calvary! What a picture of what the Lord Jesus Christ did for me, and for you.

And here is the sacred promise, "And Abraham called the name of the place, The-LORD-Will-Provide; as it is said to this day, 'In the Mount of the LORD it shall be provided" (Genesis 22:14). What shall be seen? Calvary. That is the promise.

On the mount of the Lord, in this same place, God will provide Himself a Lamb. Moriah, "foreseen of the Lord". It will be seen. Now you can understand when Jesus says, "Your father Abraham rejoiced to see My day, and he saw *it* and was glad" (John 8:56). Now you can understand what the Bible means when it says the Gospel was preached to Abraham (see Galatians 3:8). Do you think Abraham was glad that day, when Isaac got up and that ram got down? Of course he was!

The Covenant Protection

Look again at Genesis 17:8. God says, "Also I give to you and your descendants after you the land in which you are a stranger, all the land of Canaan, as an everlasting possession; and I will be their God."

God has not given up on the Jewish people. God loves them, and many of them love Him. And God says, "...I will be their God." There is a prophecy in Revelation that in the last days there is going to be a wholesale turning of God's ancient people to faith in Jesus Christ (see Revelation 4:7). I believe that Jesus is the Messiah of Israel.

We know that the world is going to face some dark days. We know there is coming a time on this earth that the Bible calls the Great Tribulation. But we also know that great good is going to come out of this tribulation.

Behold, I will make Jerusalem a cup of drunkenness to all the surrounding peoples, when they lay siege against Judah and Jerusalem. And it shall happen in that day that I will make Jerusalem a very heavy stone for all peoples; all who would heave it away will surely be cut in pieces, though all nations of the earth are gathered against it. (Zechariah 12:2-3)

It seems to me that some of our loyalties we used to have seem to be ebbing away, and the nations seem to be gathering a noose around little Israel. I want to tell you, friend: America better keep standing by Israel. God says those who bless Israel, He will bless, and those who curse Israel, He will curse.

God said all of the nations, all of the peoples of the earth are going to be gathered against Israel. Look again in Zechariah 12:3,

And it shall happen in that day that I will make Jerusalem a very heavy stone for all peoples; all who would heave it away will surely be cut in pieces, though all nations of the earth are gathered against it.

Every man, woman, boy, girl on this earth together will not set aside the decrees of God. God says, in effect, "You go against me, you're going against yourself." As Benjamin Franklin told Thomas Payne, "He that spits against the wind spits in his own face." (Franklin, Benjamin. *The Select Works of Benjamin Franklin.* Boston: Phillips, Sampson & Co. 1855.)

See what God is going to do in Zechariah 12:9, "It shall be in that day that I will seek to destroy all the nations that come against Jerusalem." And then, notice the blessed promise in Zechariah 12:10, "And I will pour on the house of David and on the inhabitants of Jerusalem the Spirit of grace...."

Do you know that you are saved by grace—or you're not saved at all? "For by grace you have been saved through faith...." (Ephesians 2:8a).

God says later in Zechariah 12:10,

And I will pour on the house of David and on the inhabitants of Jerusalem the Spirit of grace and supplication; then they will look on Me whom they pierced. Yes, they will mourn for Him as one mourns for his only son, and grieve for Him as one grieves for a firstborn.

Who is speaking in this verse? The LORD, Jehovah, is speaking. Think about this—this is an Old Testament text. How can God be pierced? I'll tell you how. God became flesh, and God hung on a cross.

The Bible speaks of the Church which God has purchased with His own blood (see Acts 20:28). Whose blood was shed upon the cross? The blood of God! God can be pierced *when God becomes a human*—when God becomes the Messiah of Israel.

"...then they will look on Me whom they pierced. Yes, they will mourn for Him as one mourns for his only son...." That is, they shall understand when the scales fall from their eyes, as they did from the eyes of the apostle Paul (see Acts 9:17-18).

I want you to see a blessed verse, Zechariah 13:1, "In that day a fountain shall be opened for the house of David and for the inhabitants of Jerusalem, for sin and for uncleanness."

> *There is a fountain filled with blood*
> *Drawn from Immanuel's veins;*
> *And sinners, plunged beneath that flood,*
> *Lose all their guilty stains.*

(From the hymn *"There Is a Fountain Filled with Blood"*; by William Cowper, 1772)

God is saying, "In that day, they will look upon Me, their Messiah." They will call out to Him, and He will hear and answer. And Paul says, "And so all Israel will be saved, as it is written: "The Deliverer will come out of Zion, And He will turn away ungodliness from Jacob" (Romans 11:26).

I thank God for this Book, the Bible. I thank God for these promises and these prophecies. As I read the newspapers and see what is happening, I can go all the way back to the Book of Genesis and see that immutable, unchangeable, irrevocable, unbreakable promise that God made to father Abraham. What a great God we have, and what great days we are living in. I believe we are living very close to the time that Zechariah was talking about. And I believe it behooves everyone reading this right now to give his or her heart to Jesus, to be saved, to trust Him, to look upon Him.

He will save you!

Chapter 3

THE CRADLE

U pon an occasion, I had an opportunity to witness to Mohammed Ali. I had prayed much about it, and God arranged so we could be together in a small room, late at night, before one of his fights. We were talking about Jesus Christ, and I had a prayer in my heart that this man might receive Christ as his personal Lord and Savior.

Mohammed Ali was studying the Islamic faith. He said, "You say that Jesus Christ is the Son of God because He was born of a virgin; He didn't have an earthly father. *Adam* didn't have a father or a mother—wouldn't that make Adam more a Son of God than Jesus?"

I said, "Champ, I want you to understand this: Jesus was not the Son of God because He was born of a virgin. He was born of a virgin because He was the Son of God."

You see, Jesus did not have His start in Bethlehem. Jesus stepped out of the glory. "For unto us a Child is born, unto us a Son is given" (Isaiah 9:6a). I am aware that the world laughs at the idea of a virgin birth; they think of it as some sort of primitive, medieval superstition or something. I can tell you, furthermore, that the devil hates the idea of the virgin birth, because it teaches both the humanity and the deity of his nemesis, our Savior, the Lord Jesus Christ.

But worse than the mockery of this world and the hatred of Satan is the ignorance of many so-called Christians concerning the virgin birth. Many of them doubt it. Some don't believe it at all. And others think it is incidental.

I want to show you that you have no hope of salvation apart from the virgin birth. I want to show you that if you take away the virgin birth of our Lord and Savior Jesus Christ, you have destroyed the whole foundation of Christianity, and it will all collapse like a house of cards. It is not incidental; it is fundamental.

The Sacred Mystery of His Birth

First of all, think of the sacred mystery of His birth. In Luke 1 the angel has announced to Mary she is going to be with child. Now, Mary is a virgin. She is espoused to a man named Joseph, but they've not come together in the act of marriage; the ceremony has not yet transpired. They are not living together as husband and wife.

Yet, the angel Gabriel says, "Mary, you are going to have a baby" (see Luke 1:30-31). Then Mary asks a very pertinent question in Luke 1:34, "Then Mary said to the angel, 'How can this be, since I do not know a man?'" Big question: "How's this going to happen? This is a mystery to me." The phrase *do not know* literally means that she has not had sexual relations with a man.

> And the angel answered and said to her, "The Holy Spirit will come upon you, and the power of the Highest will overshadow you; therefore, also, that Holy One who is to be born will be called the Son of God. Now indeed, Elisabeth your relative has also conceived a son in her old age; and this is now the sixth month for her, who was called barren. For with God nothing will be impossible." (Luke 1:35-37)

If you have difficulty with that, you are going to have difficulty with the virgin birth. "For with God nothing will be impossible. Then Mary said, 'Behold the maidservant of the Lord! Let it be to me according to your word.' And the angel departed from her" (Luke 1:37-38).

We are talking about the mystery of the virgin birth. May I tell you that the virgin birth does not depend upon your understanding for its validation? Is that okay? You don't have to understand it to validate it! There are a lot of things we don't understand.

We don't understand how a brown cow can eat green grass and give white milk, which churns into yellow butter. Most of us don't even understand how a windshield wiper works. We know *it works*—it takes the water off the windshield. But if you had to write a diagram and describe to me what makes the windshield wiper go back and forth, there are many of you who could not do it. Folks, I'm telling you there are a lot of things we don't understand, but we experience. As Vance Havner said, "I do not understand all about electricity, but I don't intend to sit in the dark until I do."

Mary asked a good question. "Then Mary said to the angel, 'How can this be, since I do not know a man?'" (Luke 1:34). There are some people who say, "Is the idea of a virgin birth not a biological impossibility?" Again, I want to tell you that it is not a biological impossibility if you let the angel answer the question. "For with God nothing will be impossible" (Luke 1:37).

The late, great Robert G. Lee, the former pastor of Bellevue Baptist Church, wrote a book, which he gave me many years ago, before I came to be the pastor of Bellevue. It is called *Lord, I Believe* and it deals with miracles. And from that book, I will quote Dr. Lee:

> *"I do not believe God is an impotent and puzzled bell-hop running up and down the corridors of the house He designed by His omniscience and created by His omnipotence, having lost the key to some of the mystery rooms of His own house. It is impossible for Him to be baffled or bothered or chained by the physical elements."*

(From the book *Lord, I Believe* by Dr. Robert G. Lee)

What Dr. Lee is saying is God is not bound by the very laws that He Himself has created in the universe that He Himself has made. He is the Master and the Lord of that universe. God can do anything He well pleases—because He is God.

I have no difficulty with the virgin birth if I believe in creation. Friend, I've often said that if you can get past Genesis 1:1, you are home free concerning miracles. "In the beginning God created the heavens and the earth." Do you have difficulty believing the virgin birth? God made the first man, without a father or a mother, from clay that He formed out of nothing. It may be a mystery to you, but it is not a mystery to God.

I love 1 Timothy 3:16, "And without controversy great is the mystery of godliness: God was manifest in the flesh, justified in the Spirit, seen by angels, preached among the Gentiles, believed on in the world, received up in glory." Now that is what the virgin birth is all about. God was manifest in the flesh, justified in the Spirit, seen by angels.

Have you ever thought about that, *"seen by angels"*? Did you know through all eternity, the eons of the ages, no angel had ever seen God? Because God is invisible. The first time any angel—or anybody—ever saw God was when the Word was made flesh. The angels said, "Look, there is God lying in a manger!"

Don't worry if you can't explain the virgin birth. You couldn't explain the virgin birth any more than you could explain God; when you can explain God, then perhaps you can explain the virgin birth. Great is the mystery of godliness. We join Mary in saying, "How can this be?" We join the angel when we say, "For with God nothing will be impossible." Settled. That's it. God did it. If you have difficulty believing the virgin birth, I'll tell you what your real difficulty is: your God is too small.

The Saving Ministry of His Birth

I want you to see the saving ministry of His birth. Let's begin with Luke 2:8-14,

> Now there were in the same country shepherds living out in the field, keeping watch over their flock by night. And behold, an angel of the Lord stood before them, and the glory of the Lord shone around them, and they were greatly afraid. Then the angel said to them, "Do not be afraid, for behold, I bring you good tidings of great joy which will be to all people. For there is born to you this day in the city of David a Savior, who is Christ the Lord. And this will be the sign to you: You will find

a Babe wrapped in swaddling cloths, lying in a manger."
And suddenly there was with the angel a multitude of
the heavenly host praising God and saying: "Glory
to God in the highest, And on earth peace, goodwill
toward men!

The virgin birth and the incarnation—that is, God being
made flesh—were necessary for our salvation.

I want you to follow me here: God gave Adam and Eve
dominion in the Garden of Eden. They sinned, and they lost that
dominion. They forfeited it. They turned it over to Satan. And
rather than being servants of God, they became slaves of Satan.
They infected the entire human race with sin. Our dominion was
lost by a man, and the only way it could ever be returned to us is by
another man, and that other man is the Lord Jesus.

All of us today are represented by one of two men; either
Adam or Jesus. "For as in Adam all die, even so in Christ all shall
be made alive" (1 Corinthians 15:22). There are really only two men
who have ever lived, and the rest of us are part and parcel of those
two men.

Jesus Christ, the last Adam, came—born of a virgin—to undo
what the first Adam did. Apart from the virgin birth, therefore, there
is no hope of salvation. How did Jesus come to undo what the first
Adam did? Well, the Bible plainly teaches, "For the wages of sin
is death" (Romans 6:23a). "The soul who sins shall die" (Ezekiel
18:20a). "Without shedding of blood there is no remission"
(Hebrews 9:22b).

Sin must be paid for. It must be atoned. And it must be atoned
for by shed blood. "God is Spirit," John 4:24 says; the great, eternal
I AM is a Spirit, and so the great and eternal I AM cannot die, and
cannot bleed. But this dominion was lost by a man, and therefore, it
must be redeemed by a man. "Without shedding of blood there is
no remission."

But not just any man will do; this man must be a perfect man.
He must be sinless, and innocent. We are all sons and daughters of
Adam by birth, and no son or daughter of Adam can qualify. Why?
Romans 5:12 says, "Therefore, just as through one man [Adam] sin

entered the world, and death through sin, and thus death spread to all men, because all sinned." (Word in brackets added for clarity)

Is there anybody reading this who would have the audacity, the unmitigated gall, to stand up and say, "I've never sinned"? Of course not. We know that we are sinners by birth, by choice, by practice, by nature. "For all have sinned and fall short of the glory of God" (Romans 3:23).

Had Jesus Christ been born like we are born, He would have been a son of Adam. Had He been a son of Adam, He would have been a sinner. Had He been a sinner, He could not have been innocent. Had He not been innocent, He could have been nobody's substitute; not mine, not yours, not anybody else's. The only sin He could die for would be His own.

God wants us saved. "For God so loved the world that He gave His only begotten Son, that whoever believes in Him should not perish but have everlasting life" (John 3:16). And so, God's answer is a man—a sinless man, a perfect man, the God-man, the Lord Jesus Christ; someone who was both truly human and fully sinless. Human, so that He might undo what the first Adam did, and sinless so that He might shed blood, the blood that must be sinless.

Whose blood was in baby Jesus? It wasn't Mary's blood. By the way, when a little baby is being carried in its mother's womb, that little baby has a separate life from the mother. There's different blood in that baby. The mother may have one blood type; the baby has another blood type. Sometimes, in a paternity suit in a court of law, a father may prove by blood tests that he did not sire a baby. How is that? Because the blood line is not determined by the mother, but by the father.

Whose blood circulated in baby Jesus? The blood of God. Now you say, "Wait a minute. You said that God doesn't have blood; God is Spirit." You're catching on! Paul is talking to the Ephesian elders in Acts 20:28, and he said, "Therefore take heed to yourselves and to all the flock, among which the Holy Spirit has made you overseers, shepherd the church of God, which He purchased with His own blood."

That is, a pastor better be careful, because he has an obligation from God. The Holy Ghost has made him an overseer, and that literally means "bishop."

The blood of God circulated through baby Jesus in His mother's womb. Sinless blood, innocent blood. If you take away the virgin birth, you have no hope of Heaven. He came as He did (born of a virgin) to be what He was (sinless). He was what He was (sinless) to do what He did (die a substitutionary death). He died a substitutionary death to atone for sin. He did what He did that we might be born again and go to Heaven. No sinless sacrifice, no atonement. No atonement, no new birth. No new birth, no new hope of Heaven.

He was born of a virgin so that we might be born again. He came to earth so that we might go to Heaven. He became the Son of man so that we might become the sons and the daughters of God. That's what it's all about. That is why we have the virgin birth. Had Jesus not been born of a virgin, He would have been a son of Adam.

Gregor Mendel, who did great work in genetics (that is, the effect of our genetic code; our DNA), said this: "Every individual is the sum total of the characteristics, recessive or dominant, in its two progenitors." Let me put that in plain English: all that was in your father and mother is in you. Not some; all. You are the sum total of the genetic characteristics of your father and mother.

Those characteristics, according to Mendel, may be recessive or dominant. It may be that they're just lying low. Your parents may have had good characteristics that are recessive in you, or they may have had bad characteristics that are recessive in you. They may have had good characteristics that are dominant or recessive in you, but it's all there in you.

Now you can understand the reason for the virgin birth. Remember, all that is in your parents is in you. Now suppose the parents of the Lord Jesus Christ had both been deity: God plus God. Then Jesus would have been fully, perfectly God, because all that was in His parents was in Him. But there would be no humanity there. He would be remote, unapproachable. There is no way He could save.

Suppose that the parents of the Lord Jesus Christ had not been God plus God, but human plus human. Then Jesus would have been fully human; He would have inherited the characteristics of His father and His mother. And, "For as in Adam all die" (1 Corinthians 15:22a), He would have been a sinner and could have been nobody's Savior.

But now let's not suppose, but learn, that His Father is truly God. His mother is truly human. Then who is He? He is God in human flesh. He is the God-man. Not half God and half man; not all God and no man; not all man and no God. He is the only begotten Son of God, and He is the only one qualified to die upon that cross for our salvation!

Never overlook, and never mock the virgin birth. Thank God that He stepped out of Heaven and was born of a virgin. Then the angel said to them, "Do not be afraid, for behold, I bring you good tidings of great joy, which will be to all people" (Luke 2:10). Jesus Christ is not the white man's Savior, the black man's Savior, the yellow man's Savior, the western Savior, or the eastern Savior. He is the Savior of the *world*.

The world needs Jesus. Jew, Gentile, young, old, rich, poor, intellectual, and illiterate, we all need Jesus. White man, black man, yellow man, red man, here, there, everywhere—this world needs Jesus, the virgin-born Son of God.

The Sovereign Majesty of His Birth

I've talked about the sacred mystery of His birth, and the saving ministry of His birth. Let me talk to you about the sovereign majesty of His birth.

> Then the angel said to her, "Do not be afraid, Mary, for you have found favor with God. And behold, you will conceive in your womb and bring forth a Son, and shall call His name JESUS. He will be great, and will be called the Son of the Highest; and the Lord God will give Him the throne of His father David. And He will reign over the house of Jacob forever, and of His kingdom there will be no end."(Luke 1:30-33)

The name *Jesus* and the Old Testament name *Joshua*—the same name—mean "Jehovah saves." Notice verses 32 and 33, talking about the sovereign majesty of this baby.

As the Son of God, He shares the nature of God; like Father, like Son. Who is this baby, virgin-born? Plain, straight, and simple, He is God in human flesh. Now, the Mormons don't accept this. They believe He is a God, but not the one true God. Jehovah's Witnesses do not accept this. Those of the Islamic faith do not accept this. The Unitarians do not accept this. The liberal theologians do not accept this.

The Bible says in Hebrews 1:8: "But to the Son He says, 'Your throne, O God, is forever and ever; a scepter of righteousness is the scepter of thy kingdom.'" This baby is as much God as if He were not man at all. He is the earthly child of a heavenly Father and the heavenly child of an earthly mother. That little baby lying in a manger, wrapped in swaddling clothes with His dimpled feet touching the straw, is the Mighty God of Genesis 1:1.

Do you believe it? I believe it. The apostle John believed it. John 1:1-3 says,

> In the beginning was the Word, and the Word was with God, and the Word was God. He was in the beginning with God. All things were made through Him, and without Him nothing was made that has been made."

The Word is another name for Jesus. He made the manger that He lay in. He is God from everlasting. Jesus did not begin with Mary in Bethlehem; He existed, ageless, with His Father in Heaven. It has been well said that when He was born, He was as ageless as His Father and older than His mother. He has come to rule and to reign.

What is the world coming to? It's coming to Jesus. His is the cradle that will rock the world. One day our dear Savior is going to step out of the glory. Those blessed nail-pierced feet will touch the Mount of Olives, and there will be a great earthquake. Jesus is going to make His way to Jerusalem, "And the government will be upon His shoulders" (Isaiah 9:6).

What is wrong with the world today? Have you read the news this morning? Yesterday? Last week? Read any news article and you know that there is something tragically wrong with our world. It looks like we're looking into the barrel of a loaded canon. There can be no real peace without the Prince of Peace. The answer to this world's problems is the Second Coming of the Lord Jesus Christ. The hope of the individual, the hope of the Church, the hope of the family, the hope of this nation, and the hope of this world is Jesus Christ.

There used to be an old English evangelist named Henry Morehouse. Henry Morehouse was a fearless preacher, and he told a story which I want to share with you. Many years ago, there was a group of men who were in the London Zoo, and they were having a little contest to see how many rats a terrier dog could kill. They were betting on this, like men bet on cock fights or horse races or dog races. They were betting on how many rats the terrier could kill in a given period of time. They took this little terrier and put him in a pen with 25 vicious rats. The terrier was killing those rats rapidly, but he didn't kill enough. His owner lost some money on him.

So his owner pulled him out of that pit and kicked and beat him mercilessly, and then in a fit of anger he took the little dog and threw him over the fence into the lion cage, thinking the lion would devour him. That old lion came over and looked at that pitiful creature, beaten and bloody. The lion just kind of nosed him and coddled him, and then put his paws over him to protect him and looked at the man who had done such a thing. The old lion had seen it all, and he was angry that such a thing had been done to another creature.

About that time the zookeeper came, and said, "Who did this? Who threw that dog in there?"

And the terrier's owner said, "Well, I did. I was just excited. I want you to get him out for me." The zookeeper acted like he didn't even hear it. The owner got belligerent again. "I said I want my dog back!"

And there was the dog, being protected by the lion. The zookeeper said, "You do? All right, I'll open the gate and let you go in and get him."

Henry Morehouse said, "You know, I was like that; beaten, bruised, maimed, and wounded by Satan and by sin. And the Lion of Judah, the Lord Jesus, has come as my Savior and my Protector."

Some time ago, a middle-aged lady received a telegram telling her that she had inherited more than a million dollars—back in the days when a million dollars was truly a million dollars. She was flabbergasted. She didn't even know that she had a relative who had that kind of money. She was so excited she didn't know what to do. She was home by herself, and she went to the telephone, picked it up, and said, "Operator! Get me somebody on the line! Anybody! I want to tell them what has happened." Shouldn't we feel that way about Jesus? Oh, I just want to tell people about the Lord Jesus Christ!

Why the virgin birth? Jesus came to earth that we might go to Heaven. The whole purpose is wrapped up in the substitutionary death. The Bible says, "All we like sheep have gone astray; we have turned, every one, to his own way; and the LORD has laid on Him the iniquity of us all" (Isaiah 53:6).

You know that the Bible says, "For the wages of sin is death, but the gift of God is eternal life in Christ Jesus our Lord" (Romans 6:23). You know that you are doomed for eternity without Christ if something is not done about your sin, because there is one thing God will not do: He will never overlook your sin. Is this getting through to you?

There you are, and there's your sin. Here is Jesus, virgin-born, the sinless Son of God! No taint in Him, no sin in Him, no blame on Him. The Bible says, "And the LORD has laid on him the iniquity of us all." Our sins are laid on Jesus. The sinless One carried those sins to the cross. And in agony and blood, He died upon that cross to pay our sin debt. Because our sin is on Jesus, thank God, His righteousness is on us. That's good news. And the Bible says it clearly, plainly, simply, sweetly, and sublimely, "So they said, 'Believe on the Lord Jesus Christ, and you will be saved, you and your household'" (Acts 16:31).

Chapter 4

THE CUP

To the east of the city of Jerusalem, there's a little mountain called the Mount of Olives. It's a limestone ridge about 300 feet above the city of Jerusalem, about a mile in length, and about 2,700 feet above sea level. And on the western slope of the Mount of Olives is a garden.

If you go to Israel today, you can visit that garden; I have visited it many times. And in that garden, there are some beautiful shrubs, primarily olive trees. As a matter of fact, eight ancient olive trees stand there—some believe they go back to the time of Christ. Their massive trunks are knotted and gnarled, and they stand like silent sentinels, watching over that garden where Jesus came to pray—for we believe that it is the exact spot where He prayed. Tradition, all the way back to the second century, says *this is the place*: it's Gethsemane.

The word *Gethsemane* literally means "oil press," and it was in this garden that they had a giant press to squeeze the oil from the olives. Jesus would often come to this place, and He would kneel and pray.

But this night was like no other night. Jesus had been up on Mount Zion. There, in an upper room, He had the last supper with His disciples. He talked about His coming crucifixion and, prior to that, His betrayal. Judas had gone away in the darkness to do that dastardly deed.

Then the Lord Jesus, needing prayer, left Mount Zion, and He came down and crossed a brook. The brook was Kidron, and scholars tell us that when they would make animal sacrifices on the Temple Mount, the blood would run down into the brook Kidron, and it would literally be crimson with blood.

When Jesus left that upper room and came down and crossed the valley to go up to the garden, He had to cross that brook running crimson with blood. Surely it must have reminded the Lord Jesus that soon His blood would flow in that same spot from Moriah, the Temple Mount.

But Jesus came to this garden. He kneeled at that rock of agony, and He prayed. Three times Jesus prayed, "Lord, if it be possible, let this cup pass from Me" (See Luke 22:42; Matthew 26:39). Now He wasn't talking about a literal cup like you can hold in your hand. He was using a metaphor, a figure of speech, a symbol, one which meant *to experience something fully*, to take something into one's very being, as one would take a cup and put it to one's lips. And Jesus said, "Father, please, if it be possible, let this cup pass from Me."

It was the cup of agony Jesus drank in dark Gethsemane, and He drank it there alone.

Do you know when the Lord Jesus began His ministry, when He was performing miracles, when He was feeding the multitudes, opening blind eyes, healing withered limbs, how the crowds followed Him? Oh, they loved the miracles He did. But when Jesus Christ began to speak to them of deeper eternal verities and full surrender to His lordship, they began to leave Him. As a matter of fact, they left in droves.

The Lord Jesus had to turn to His disciples and say, "Will you also go away?" And from multitudes, now He has just twelve. But now, one of the twelve has left; Judas has gone to betray Him. Now He has only eleven. But out of that eleven, He chooses a trinity of disciples to come and watch and pray with Him. Now He has three. But those three failed Him; they're asleep.

And now He goes to Gethsemane. Only Jesus the Son and God the Father are there. But in Gethsemane, Jesus knows that soon, God the Father must turn His back on Him. And Jesus will drink that cup alone—alone in Gethsemane.

Let's look at Luke 22, beginning in verse 39.

> Coming out, He went to the Mount of Olives, as He was accustomed, and His disciples also followed Him. When He came to the place, He said to them, "Pray that you may not enter into temptation." And He was withdrawn from them about a stone's throw, and He knelt down and prayed, saying, "Father, if it is Your will, take this cup away from Me; nevertheless not My will, but Yours, be done." Then an angel appeared to Him from heaven, strengthening Him. And being in agony, He prayed more earnestly. Then His sweat became like great drops of blood falling down to the ground. When He rose up from prayer, and had come to His disciples, He found them sleeping from sorrow. Then He said to them, "Why do you sleep? Rise and pray, lest you enter into temptation." (vv. 39-46)

Then the story goes on to tell how Judas came and betrayed the Son of God with a kiss.

The Contents of the Cup

I want us to think now about the cup that Jesus drank in the garden of Gethsemane. I want us to think about the contents of the cup. What was in that cup that was so loathsome, so terrifying? Yes, *terrifying*—because you're going to see that Jesus shrank in horror from it. What was so vile, so filthy that the very Son of God shrank back in dread? What were the contents of that cup?

Was it physical death by crucifixion that caused such dread? Indeed it might cause such dread, because never has a form of execution been known to man that was more ignominiously painful, hurtful, and shameful than death by crucifixion.

But others had died that way and other martyrs had gone to their death, and not with dread, but saying, "Gladly will I fling my body in the grave for the Lord Jesus Christ." It wasn't physical death that He shrank back from; not even the pains of a crucifixion.

Was it some extraordinary attack of Satan? Is that what Jesus shrank back from? No.

Jesus had already met Satan in the wilderness. He'd already conquered Satan. Satan still hounded Him all the way to the cross, but Jesus had no fear of Satan, and no dread of Satan. He said, "Now is the judgment of this world: now the ruler of this world will be cast out" (John 12:31).

What was it that was breaking the heart of the Lord Jesus Christ? Was it the betrayal of Judas? Was it the failure of the disciples? Yes, he was disappointed. But there's a difference in disappointment and dread.

So *what was it* that caused Jesus to dread the drinking of that cup? What was *in* that cup?

The Pollution of Sin Was in That Cup

The Bible says in Hebrews 4:15 that Jesus was tempted in all points, as we are, and yet He was without sin. But the Bible also teaches us that in order for the Lord Jesus Christ to redeem us, our sin had to be placed upon Him. And 2 Corinthians 5:21 says this, "For He made Him who knew no sin to be sin for us, that we might become the righteousness of God in Him."

Do you know what was in that cup? The sin of the ages was in that cup. My sin and your sin was in that cup. Suppose we were to go through the world today and put my sin in it, and yours, and his, and hers, and theirs…and put it right in there.

Not some of your sin—*all* of your sin. Every vile thought; every wicked deed; every hurtful, hateful thing. All of the sin of the churches, and then the sin of the cities, and then the sin of this nation, and then the sin of this world.

Now put it in the cup and take all the sins of the past and all of the sins of the future, distill it, and put it in this cup. Put rape in there. Put sodomy in there. Put child abuse in there. Put Hitler's gas ovens in there. Put murder in there. Put blasphemy in there. Put witchcraft in there. Put filth in there and say, "Jesus, drink it. Drink it. Drink the bitter dregs. Don't just bear sin, but *become* sin."

I didn't say Jesus sinned; *He* never sinned. But He was made sin for us, because He carried that sin to the cross.

You may not understand what sin is, but I can tell you Jesus Christ knew what sin is.

Jesus had seen sin turn angels into demons and men into beasts. Sin is a clenched fist in the face of God. And Jesus knew that when He drank that cup, He would be numbered with the transgressors—the sinners. And Him whose name is Holy, who is the complete antithesis of sin, would become sin.

The Punishment of Sin Was in That Cup

Jesus knew that the punishment—not of some sin, but of all sin; not of some people, but of all people—would be upon Him.

One man, the God-man, would bear it all, and when He did, God the Father would have to treat Him as if He had committed the sins of the people—*all* of the sins of *all* of the people. That is the reason why the Bible says in Romans 8:32 that God spared not His own son. In Isaiah 53:10, the Bible says that it pleased the Lord to bruise Him.

When Jesus took my sin and your sin, God the Father—in justice—had to treat Him as He would treat me, and as He would treat you. And Jesus knew He was going to suffer the very fires of hell.

The pains of hell were getting hold of the Lord Jesus Christ, and Jesus was going to baptize His soul in hell. Jesus was going to walk the burning corridors of the damned. Jesus was going to receive the thunderbolts of God's wrath, and Jesus Christ, the eternal Son who had been in the bosom of the Father from eternity, was going to be now separated from God on that cross. He was going to cry out, "My God, My God, why have You forsaken Me?" (Matthew 27:46; Mark 15:34).

The answer is that God is of purer eyes than to behold iniquity and God the Father *had* to turn His back on God the Son.

I said before, and you listen well, that at the cross, the sins of the world were distilled and the eternities were compressed. And

Jesus, being infinite, bore in a finite period of time what we, being finite, would bear in an infinite period of time. I'm telling you that Jesus Christ suffered an eternity of hell on that cross.

The price that Jesus paid only the damned in hell can begin to know, but they'll never know because they're only paying *their* sin. He paid all of the sin, of all of the people, for all time.

Friend, if that doesn't move your heart, your heart is harder than a rock. That is the content of that cup. No wonder Jesus said, "O My Father, if it is possible, let this cup pass from Me..." (Matthew 26:39).

The Consumption of the Cup

But I want you to not only notice the content of that cup, I want you to notice the consumption of the cup.

The Lord Jesus drank it to the bitter dregs. Did He shrink back? Yes, He shrank back. Does that make you think less of Him? It makes me think *more* of Him. And I'll tell you why: this was not some charade. This was real. If you don't understand why He shrank back, you don't know what was in there.

In His humanity and in His holiness, seeing the vileness and the filth of sin, He said, "O God...if there be some other way!" And the silence from heaven said, "There is no other way." So, in His holy humanity, He shrank back. But in His divine love He said, "...nevertheless not my will, but Yours, be done" (Luke 22:42).

You see, Jesus paid a price. You will never know the agony that the Son of God endured there on the cross. He didn't have to die; He had a choice. Jesus Christ said:

> Therefore My Father loves Me, because I lay down My life that I may take it again. No one takes it from Me, but I lay it down of Myself. I have power to lay it down, and I have power to take it again. This command I have received from My Father. (John 10:17-18)

Jesus was the only man who ever *chose* to die. The wages of sin is death. There was no sin in Him, so there would have been no death in Him. You say, "Well, someone who commits suicide chooses to die." No he doesn't. He just chooses to die a little sooner. "And as it is appointed for men to die once, but after this the judgment" (Hebrews 9:27). Jesus was the only man who could say, "No [man] takes My life from Me. I lay it down Myself."

Jesus said, "...nevertheless not My will, but Yours, be done" (Luke 22:42b). If you'll read in Isaiah 14, of when Satan became Satan, it says, "For you have said in your heart: 'I will ascend into heaven, I will exalt my throne above the stars of God...'" (Isaiah 14:13a). Satan said this to God the Father: "Not your will, but *mine* be done." But Jesus, though He was God, said in His humanity, "Not My will, but *Yours* be done."

Adam, following Satan in the Garden of Eden, said, "Not Your will, but mine," and ruined the race. Jesus, the last Adam, said in another garden, "Not My will, but Yours," and redeemed the race. That's the consumption of the cup. The Lord Jesus willingly, voluntarily, vicariously, victoriously said, "Not My will, but Yours."

Had He said *no*, every one of us would have burned in hell forever. Had He said *no*, all of those who had already gone to the place of redemption where Jesus had promised to pay would have had to come out and go to hell.

But Jesus said, "Not My will, but Yours be done." It is because Jesus suffered, bled, and died on that cross that you and I can be redeemed—because Jesus took my sin and your sin and carried it to the cross.

Now pay attention. I want you to get this in your heart, so don't miss it. God will never overlook sin. He *cannot*. God is holy, and by His holiness He has sworn that sin will be punished.

All sin is punished. No sin goes unpunished. If God were to let one half of one sin go unpunished, God would no longer be holy. The chief attribute of God is not love; it is holiness. He is infinite, measureless, and spotless in His holiness. And God must punish sin. If He did not punish sin He would topple from His throne of holiness.

The cross is God's way to punish sin and forgive the sinner at the same time, and that is by having an innocent, sinless sin-bearer to take that sin and carry it to the cross. "For He made Him who knew no sin to be sin for us, that we might become the righteousness of God in Him" (2 Corinthians 5:21).

The Communion of the Cup

But there is another cup. This one *we* drink, and that is the Lord's Supper.

Just before Jesus went into Gethsemane, in this same chapter of Luke 22, it tells how He was at that Last Supper with His disciples. He told them, "This cup is the new covenant in My blood, which is shed for you" (Luke 22:20). Because you see, He drank the cup of sin so that we might have the cup of redemption.

There was the content of that cup, and there was the consumption of that cup, but thank God there's the communion of the cup. Thank God, because *He* drank this cup, *we* drink this cup. We drink the cup of communion because we meet Jesus there. He takes your sin. He drinks it down. You take His righteousness; you drink it down. Isn't that wonderful? Amen!

> God forbid that we should fail to be moved by Gethsemane when you think of the words that are used in all of the Gospels to talk about what the Lord Jesus Christ bore, such as, "Then He said to them, 'My soul is exceeding sorrowful, even unto death…'" (Matthew 26:38).

Had not an angel come to minister to Him, He would have died there. When He perspired, the sweat was like blood. It *was* blood, because the minute capillaries had ruptured. He was in such extreme distress that blood was dripping from His brow.

Sometimes Jesus would pray standing; sometimes Jesus would lift His face to heaven to pray. Sometimes, Jesus would kneel to pray, but in Gethsemane, He fell on His face.

Can you imagine what He must have looked like when Judas led that group into the garden? Can you see Him? His face is matted; red blood and black dirt on His face. His heart is broken. This is the way they found Him when Judas planted that kiss of shame upon the Lord Jesus Christ.

Jesus said, "My soul is exceeding sorrowful." The word *sorrowful* has the idea of being separated, alone. Before those nails ever went into the hands of Jesus, they had already come into His soul. Gethsemane was the vestibule of Calvary. The victory was really won in Gethsemane, not on Calvary. It was *paid for* at Calvary; it was *won* in Gethsemane.

Knowing what He would go through, there is another word Jesus used when He said, "exceeding sorrowful." That word, *exceeding*, has the idea of being surrounded with no way out, no escape, no hope; absolute abject suffering. Jesus paid that for me and for you.

But in our text, Jesus spoke of His agony. Do you know what *agony* means? Why do they call that place where He prayed "the rock of agony"? The *agon* was an athletic contest in Greece. It was a wrestling match. Jesus was wrestling; He was in *agony*.

Was He wrestling with God the Father? No, never! The great desire of His heart was to please the Father. Was He wrestling with Satan? He never needed to. He had absolute authority over Satan. So who was He wrestling with? With Himself. There was His holy humanity, and there was His divine love. And so there was that contest, that wrestling.

I'm glad His love won, aren't you? I'm glad love paid the price in dark Gethsemane!

There is a story that comes down to us through the ages. It's been told so many times that it must be rooted into history. It is said Nero had forty men in his army who were wrestlers. They were gladiators who would come to the field of endeavor, to the *agon*, to wrestle for Nero. And they wanted to please their emperor.

As these forty wrestlers would come to wrestle before him, the Emperor would sit in his finery, in his velvet-draped box, upon his throne, and he would watch the games as these wrestlers would wrestle. They were the finest athletes in all of Rome. They would come out with their square shoulders and bulging biceps, look up into the box of their Emperor, and they would chant, *"We are forty wrestlers wrestling for thee, O Emperor, to win for thee the victory, and for thee the victor's crown!"*

Everybody in the empire knew who these wrestlers were. They were the counterpart of our Olympic champions today.

But then word came to Nero that some in the army had become Christians. Christianity was beginning to spread. To be a Christian now was a crime worthy of death; Christians were to be put to death by fire, by sword, or by beast. And so Nero sent out a word to his commander-in-chief, Vespasian, and said, "You need to go through the ranks of your troops. If you find any Christians, they shall be executed."

So Vespasian lined his troops up and he said, "An edict has come from the Emperor, that should there be any Christians, I'm to ask them to confess to being a Christian. I am told that a Christian will never deny that he is a Christian. But I want to say before you confess, that if you are a Christian, and if you do confess, you will surely be put to death." Then Vespasian said, "Are there any Christians?"

He wasn't prepared for what was about to happen.

As if they were one man, forty men stepped forward. All forty of those wrestlers had given their hearts and their lives to Jesus Christ.

When Vespasian saw that, he said, "No, no. There's some mistake. Not you forty!" But every man of them said, "We believe that Jesus Christ is the Son of God."

Vespasian said, "Please step back…step back! Renounce your faith and it will be over." But not one of them moved. Vespasian said, "I cannot put you to death with a sword. I believe you've not thought it through. Surely you will renounce your faith." Then he said, "I have a plan…"

Now it was in the middle of winter. Vespasian built a fire on a frozen lake, a big roaring fire. Then he took from those forty men their helmets, their breastplates, their greaves of brass, their shoes, their shirts, even their undergarments. He stripped them down to absolutely nothing in that sub-zero weather and then turned them away into the darkness and said, "You will stay out in the darkness until you freeze." But, he said, "If any of you out there in the cold and the darkness decides you want to renounce Christ, all you have to do is come to the fire."

Thinking surely they would come to the fire, Vespasian sent them out there and the forty men went. But he wasn't prepared for what he was about to hear. He heard the chant that he'd heard so many times…but now it was different.

This was what they were chanting: "*We are forty wrestlers, wrestling for Thee, O Christ, to win for Thee the victory and for Thee the victor's crown!*"

Vespasian said, "Well, they're chanting now, but they will soon change." But on through the night, as the cold grew deeper, they heard this chant. *"Forty wrestlers wrestling for Thee, O Christ, to win for Thee the victory and for Thee the victor's crown!"* The chant grew weaker... and weaker...and weaker. They were being numbed by the cold.

Just then the chanting stopped, and Vespasian looked. There, slithering across the ice, was the naked form of one of those soldiers, turning his back on Jesus Christ to come to the fire. And Vespasian said, "Ha-ha! Here he comes. The rest will soon follow. I knew it. I know men. The others will be coming soon."

But he wasn't prepared for what he was about to hear.

He listened, and he heard in the darkness, *"Thirty-nine wrestlers, wrestling for Thee, O Christ, to win for Thee the victory and for Thee the victor's crown!"*

When Vespasian heard that, he looked at the miserable form before him slithering on the ice, and according to the story the way I heard it, Vespasian took his own helmet from his head; from his chest, his armor; from his back, his shirt; from his feet, his shoes; and Vespasian ran toward the thirty-nine, saying, *"Forty wrestlers wrestling for Thee, O Christ, to win for Thee the victory and for Thee the victor's crown!"*

Jesus wrestled for me; I want to wrestle for Him. Don't you?

Am I a soldier of the cross? I want to be. As I look at dark Gethsemane, I tell you, there are two things that it tells me.

Number one, I want to hate sin.

Number two, I want to love Jesus Christ. And so should every one of us.

Chapter 5

THE CROWN

The Lord Jesus was crowned with thorns. It was not incidental, nor was it accidental, that Jesus was crowned with thorns.

The idea of crowning Him with thorns came from a diseased mind. The crowning with thorns was a cruel mockery; it was a wicked act of hatred and rebellion. And yet, in another sense, Jesus being crowned with thorns was a part of a drama that had been written before the world was swung into space. Jesus being crowned with thorns has a message, a message indescribably glorious and wonderful.

We can see earlier in Matthew 27 how Jesus came into Pilate's judgment hall, and Pilate tried to wash his hands of making a decision and allowed Jesus to be scourged. They tied Him to a whipping post, and then they took a vicious whip to Him that cut His back to ribbons. Men would have died from that kind of scourging, had they not been strong.

When they had finished, they put a scarlet robe on Him, and they put a bamboo reed in His hand for a scepter. They took a crown of thorns and pressed it on His brow and then they took clubs and beat him on His head. No rubies were in this crown. The only rubies there were the ruby red drops of the blood of the Son of God.

Speaking of Pilate, the Bible says beginning in Matthew 27:26:

> Then he released Barabbas to them; and when he had scourged Jesus, he delivered Him to be crucified. Then the soldiers of the governor took Jesus into the Praetorium and gathered the whole garrison around Him. And they stripped Him and put a scarlet robe on Him. When they had twisted a crown of thorns, they put it on His head, and a reed in His right hand. And they bowed the knee before Him and mocked Him, saying, "Hail, King of the Jews!" Then they spat on Him, and took the reed and struck Him on the head. And when they had mocked Him, they took the robe off Him, put His own clothes on Him, and led Him away to be crucified. (vv. 26-31)

Are you ready for some wonderful truths? Do you want to see why I said this was not incidental, and not accidental, that God allowed this to happen? And how, though done by the hands of wicked men, this was yet a part of the magnificent plan of Almighty God?

There are several things I want you to notice.

The Sacred Mystery of the Crown

In one sense, this was the random thought, the cruel jest, the hollow mockery of a psychopathic Roman soldier. And yet on the other hand, there was a mystery here, known in the heart and mind of God.

What does a crown of thorns speak of? It symbolizes the curse that is upon humanity—on you, on me, on us all—because of sin.

When God created mankind, God put mankind in a garden. And in the Garden of Eden, there were no thorns. There were no thistles. There were no brambles. The first rose that ever bloomed was a rose that bloomed without thorns. And when Adam picked blackberries, he didn't have to fight brambles like we do to get to them. There were no thorns there.

In Genesis 3:17, our Lord speaks of the curse that came upon Adam and Eve because they sinned, because they disobeyed God. The Bible says as a result of that sin, God came into the garden. Read what God said in Genesis 3:17-18:

> Then to Adam He said, "Because you have heeded the voice of your wife, and have eaten from the tree of which I commanded you, saying, 'You shall not eat of it': "Cursed is the ground for your sake; In toil you shall eat of it all the days of your life. Both thorns and thistles it shall bring forth for you, and you shall eat the herb of the field.

Thorns and thistles began to grow on planet earth. Until this time, they had not grown. The thorn and the thistle are the sign of the curse of sin upon humanity. Hebrews 6:8 says, "but if it bears thorns and briers, it is rejected and near to being cursed, whose end is to be burned."

Jesus was bearing those thorns. Jesus was wearing that crown. Had Adam not sinned, thorns would never have grown on this earth. Jesus wore the crown of thorns because He bore the curse. The thorns Jesus wore on His head speak of the hardship, the sorrow, and the death that comes with sin.

Are you having heartaches? Are you having sorrow? Do you know sickness? I tell you this: the thorny pathway that we walk is because of sin. The bed of briars we sleep on is because of sin. And no matter how healthy you may be (or think you are) right now, and no matter how you may feather your nest, there's a thorn in it and sooner or later you'll find it.

When you go out into the field to work, no matter what your occupation is, you'll be working in a thorny field and your body will, like the apostle Paul, find a thorn in the flesh. You will know sickness, you will know suffering, you will know pain, because something has happened to Creation. Put the reference to this verse down in your margin as well: Romans 8:22, "For we know that the whole creation groans and labors with birth pangs together until now."

Why? Because there's a curse upon everything—because of sin. Do you want to know why we have confusion, frustration, suffering? Look at every hospital and say, "Sin did this." Look at every mental institution and say, "Sin did this." Look at every jail and say, "Sin did this." Look at every twisted and warped body and say, "Sin did this."

Look at all heartache, pain, toil, and anguish, and over it all you can write one word: *sin*. And the thorn is the emblem, the symbol, of that sin.

When Jesus died on that cross He was crowned with thorns. He wore the crown because He bore the curse.

The Solemn Misery of the Crown

That crown speaks of suffering, and it speaks of pain. That crown was placed upon His head over the temples, which is one of the most sensitive parts of the human body. These great spikes were put there and then on top of that, with a club they began to beat and batter the head of the Lord Jesus Christ.

Those who paint and depict the Lord Jesus on the cross are kind. We would not want to see a picture that portrayed Him literally. His face was so brutalized, you could not tell whether it was the face of a man or an animal. Remember, with their hands they had snatched the beard from His face (Isaiah 50:6).

Can you imagine that? With their fists, they had battered His face and loosened His teeth so that blood ran down from His nostrils, and it mingled with the filthy spittle from their mouths. You would not want to see Him. Isaiah 52:14 says this, "So His visage was marred more than any man, And His form more than the sons of men." That is, He didn't look like a man. He didn't even seem human, there upon the cross.

Why is this? Well, Isaiah 53:4 says, "Surely He has borne our griefs and carried our sorrows; Yet we esteemed Him stricken, smitten by God, and afflicted."

Some years ago in New York City, there was a mother who was hanging out her clothes outside. A neighbor came screaming and said, "Your house is on fire! Your house is on fire!" She dropped her clothes and ran into the house. It was a raging inferno. She went to the crib where her little girl was. She took that baby, wrapped the baby in a blanket, and came out to the front yard and laid that child upon the grass as the house was consumed. There was no chance for her to get anything else.

That mother's face took the heat of those flames and was horribly scarred. Her hands were burned, gnarled, and could never again be the kind of hands that God created them to be. But the little baby was not touched at all by the fire. Not a hair was singed. That little girl grew up to be a beautiful girl.

When she was eighteen, her high-school class was having an outing for senior day. They were on the Hudson River on a boat, and the parents had been invited. And this girl, because of her charm and her beauty, was the center of attention.

At a certain moment this girl's mother passed by, with her face hideously scarred, her hands gnarled and burned. One of the high-school girls, not thinking how cruel the remark would be, said "Who is that hideous woman?" This girl said, "I don't know." *Her own daughter* said, "I don't know who she is." She was ashamed of her mother. And her mother heard.

Later on when they got home, the mother said, "Darling, come here. I want to tell you something. You've often asked me about the burns on my hands and the burns on my face and I've never told you because I did not want to add to your sorrow and give you a burden to bear. But now I'm going to tell you. When you were a baby, I went into a burning house and rescued you. Not a hair on your head was touched, but these scars on my face and these scars on my hands are there because I rescued you from the flames."

When the daughter saw and heard that, she was smitten with shame and remorse. She took those two hands of that darling mother, put those hands together, brought them to her lips and wet them with her kisses. Then she brought that scarred face to her lips and kissed that face over and over again and said "Oh, my mother, can you ever forgive me?"

Friend, I had rather be that daughter, ashamed of her mother, than to be ashamed of Jesus who wore that crown for me.

Oh how could we ever, how could we *ever* blush to speak His name or to own His cause! For Jesus wore my crown. He bore the curse and He suffered our hell. The Bible says in 1 Peter 3:18, "For Christ also suffered once for sins, the just for the unjust, that He might bring us to God, being put to death in the flesh but made alive by the Spirit…"

The Shameful Mockery of the Crown

What were the Roman soldiers doing? Look in Matthew 27:29:

"When they had twisted a crown of thorns, they put it on His head, and a reed in His right hand. And they bowed the knee before Him and mocked Him, saying, "Hail, King of the Jews!"

Why were they mocking Him? Because of their rebellion. They were saying, "You're not our king; You're not a true king. We will not bow the knee to You." What they were doing was ridiculing His right to rule.

They didn't put a purple robe on Him—that's the sign of royalty. They put a red robe on Him—that's the symbol of sin. They did not put a scepter in His hand; they put a reed in His hand. They did not put a diadem on His brow. They put a crown of jagged thorns on His brow! And the homage that they paid Him was to spit in His face.

Can you imagine? Here is the Lord of Glory, and they spit in His face! May I tell you what the root of all sin is? It is not what you do wrong that you ought not to do, and not that you fail to do what you ought to do.

Sin is refusing to bow the knee to your rightful king. These other things are the result of that. Do you know what sin is? Sin is rebellion. Sin is a clinched fist in the face of God.

Now I want you to look at Psalms 2:1-3:

Why do the nations rage, And the people plot a vain thing? The kings of the earth set themselves, And the rulers take counsel together, Against the LORD and

against His Anointed, saying, "Let us break Their bonds
in pieces And cast away Their cords from us."

Do you know what rage is? Rage is what you do when you
don't know the answer. "And the rulers take counsel together,
Against the LORD and against His Anointed"—that means against
His Christ—"saying, 'Let us break Their bonds in pieces And cast
away Their cords from us.'"

We do not want Christ to rule over us.

When Jesus Christ came into this world, He came into the
Roman world of government, into the Greek world of culture,
and into the Hebrew world of religion. Those were the dominant
thoughts, and they rejected Him. Rather than crowning Him with a
diadem, they crowned Him with thorns.

Today the same thing is happening. In the world of government
in America, we've outlawed the Lord Jesus Christ—America, which
has had a Christian-Judeo foundation. We move from one dilemma
to another, one crisis to another, and leave standing outside the door
the only One who can unscramble the whole mess.

And in the world of culture, can you imagine standing up in
one of our great universities today and saying that "Jesus Christ is
the answer"? Oh, there is room for humanism in the universities.
There is room for blasphemy. There is room for fornication, for
sodomy, for adultery—but no room for the Lord Jesus Christ. The
so-called culture of our day has dropped beneath the dignity of the
beast of the field.

And in the world of religion, we will not bow the knee to
Jesus Christ. Many churches in the world today are glorified country
clubs with steeples on top. And the Lord Jesus Christ, crowned with
thorns, is left standing outside the door.

How many churches today are still preaching the Book, the
blood, and the blessed hope of the second coming of our Lord
and Savior Jesus Christ? You say, "Well at least they are religious."
I remind you that it was a religious crowd that crucified the Lord
Jesus Christ.

Most of the people in America don't need religion—they
need to turn from religion to Jesus Christ!

Friend, there was the *mystery* of that crown—He was wearing the curse. There was the *misery* of that crown—He suffered for us. There is the *mockery* of that crown—men today, as then, refuse to bow the knee to Jesus Christ. And today you will either bow the knee or crown Him with thorns one more time.

The Saving Ministry of the Crown

This is not by happenstance. Why did Jesus wear a crown of thorns? Because God is teaching a lesson.

He who knew no sin—that's Jesus—God had made to be sin for us. Second Corinthians 5:21 tells us, "For He made Him who knew no sin to be sin for us, that we might become the righteousness of God in Him."

What does that mean? It means that my crown of thorns, my sin, and my curse was put on the head of the Lord Jesus Christ and Jesus bore that punishment.

Please listen to me. *You are a sinner, and your sin will be punished.* God is a holy God, and God has sworn by His holiness that all sin will be punished. God never has, God never can, God never will let one half of one sin go unpunished.

Your sin *must* be punished. There's only one question: who will bear that punishment, you or Jesus? That's the only question. Sin will be pardoned in Christ or punished in hell, but sin will never be overlooked.

That's the reason the Bible says He made Him who knew no sin to be sin for us. Jesus took our sin, He was crowned with our sin, and He, the Lord Jesus, carried that sin to the cross.

Do you know where this happened? Do you know where Jesus Christ was crowned with thorns? It was Calvary. It was Golgotha. It was Mount Moriah. Mount Moriah, the Temple Mount, and Calvary are all the same limestone ridge, all the same mountain.

Centuries before Jesus Christ was born, God told Abraham to take his son, that he loves, and to offer his son as a sacrifice (Genesis 22:1-18). So Abraham and Isaac go to the place of sacrifice. Isaac knows they are going to make a sacrifice, so he looks around and says, "Father, here's the wood to burn the sacrifice. Here's the fire to start the sacrifice. We've got the rope. We've got the knife. But Father, where's the lamb?"

Abraham chokes back the tears, because Isaac does not yet know, and he says, "Son, God will provide Himself a lamb."

And up that mountain they go. The wood is put in place and Abraham must now say to his son, "You must trust me, oh my son. You must understand…I don't understand! I just believe God. I've got to do this; I don't know why. God will just have to raise you from the dead. But son, *you're* the sacrifice. Put out your hands. I must tie you."

Now by this time, Isaac was a strapping, strong young man. And that son, strong and strapping, who could have overcome Abraham who was well over a hundred years of age, willingly submits and becomes a picture of the Lord Jesus Christ. Isaac stretches out there on that altar, and Abraham lifts that gleaming knife into the sky to plunge it…when he hears a voice.

"Abraham, Abraham, do not lay your hand on the lad. I have provided a substitute" (See vv. 11-13). Abraham looked over, and there was a ram caught in a thicket—the Hebrew word there means a thicket of thorns. The ram's head was caught in the brambles, in the thorns. And God tells Abraham to take that ram and sacrifice him instead.

That ram caught in a thicket—that ram crowned with thorns—became the sacrifice that day in the place of the one who should have been and would have been sacrificed. No wonder Jesus said, "Your father Abraham rejoiced to see My day: and he saw it and was glad" (John 8:56).

God preached the gospel to Abraham so long ago, and why? Here's one sacrifice, but he gets up because there's another sacrifice crowned with thorns. And that's the saving ministry of the crown.

Abraham built many altars. You follow the life of Abraham, and you'll find the trail is dotted with altars. But he never built another altar after this episode. Why? Because this was the perfect altar, because it pictured the perfect sacrifice.

And I'll tell you something else: after Jesus Christ died upon that cross there was no need for any other altar. "For by one offering He has perfected forever them that are sanctified" (Hebrews 10:14).

And to build another altar is blasphemy. It is finished; it is done; it is paid in full.

> *Jesus paid it all,*
> *All to Him I owe;*
> *Sin had left a crimson stain,*
> *He washed it white as snow.*

(From the hymn *"Jesus Paid It All"*; Elvina M. Hall, 1865)

He was bearing our curse when He carried our sins to the cross, and when He was wearing a crown of thorns. The wickedness, the vileness, the filth of our sin, the same sin that He drank from the cup of Gethsemane, He now wore on His head as He went to Calvary.

The Sovereign Majesty of the Crown

Do you think Jesus died as a helpless victim? Do you think Jesus died because things got out of control? Do you think perhaps Satan was on the throne and Satan was doing all of this?

Let me show you a passage: Acts 4:27-28. The apostles are preaching after the resurrection of Jesus Christ, and they're seeing now with eyes washed with tears and with revelation faith. And speaking to those who crucified Jesus, they are saying:

> For truly against Your holy Servant Jesus, whom You anointed, both Herod and Pontius Pilate, with the Gentiles and the people of Israel, were gathered together to do whatever Your hand and Your purpose determined before to be done.

Now verse 27 is for man's side, but look in verse 28: "…to do whatever Your hand and Your purpose determined before to be done." Not incidental, not accidental, but a drama fulfilled in the heart and mind of God.

What am I saying? Friend, when Jesus wore this crown, He was the sovereign Majesty, not a helpless victim. What God ordained ahead of time would be done. He was in perfect control.

Crowns have always been a symbol of authority. Charlemagne wore a crown. Historians call him Charlemagne the Great. He had an octagonal crown. On each side was a plaque of gold, rubies, emeralds, and diamonds encrusted in the crown of Charlemagne the Great. It was worth a king's ransom.

Richard the Lionheart had a crown that was so heavy that when he wore his crown, there were two attendants on either side to hold his head up straight.

The Queen of England has a crown. If you've ever seen the Crown Jewels, you'll understand how magnificent that crown is.

Jesus, in Heaven, wears a crown—a crown of peace, a crown of righteousness, a crown of glory. But before He wore that crown, He wore the crown of thorns. His crown of thorns has more value than that of Charlemagne the Great, Richard the Lionheart, or the Queen of England. He wore that crown for me and for you. Oh the sovereign majesty of that crown! The rubies are the drops of His blood!

You have a choice today. Do you know what your choice is?

You can bow the knee and honor Jesus, or you can say, "Take that crown from off His head and put it on mine. I will bear my own curse. I will pay for my own sin. I will suffer and burn in hell because I refuse to bow the knee to the One who loves me so." And that is your choice.

Jesus offers to you amazing grace and wonderful love, and you can be saved. There is the mystery of this crown, there is the misery of this crown, there is the mockery of this crown, there is the ministry of this crown, and there is the majesty of this crown. I, for one, want to bow my knee and say, "All hail King Jesus!"

Hallelujah, what a Savior!

Chapter 6

THE CROSS

W hat was the reason for the cross? What was the *necessity* of the cross? I can give it to you in one word, and that one word is *sin*. If you pick up the newspapers today, you read of arson, rape, pillage, war, pornography, and disaster—but you never read the word sin.

Life is short, death is sure; sin the curse, Christ the cure. And how does Christ cure? Through His cross. Listen to this scripture, 1 Peter 3:18, "For Christ also suffered once for sins, the just for the unjust, that He might bring us to God, being put to death in the flesh but made alive by the Spirit."

Is that not a great verse? There is enough gospel dynamite in that one verse to blow the sin, hatred, sorrow, and sickness out of anybody's life. But that dynamite must be ignited by the spark of faith.

I want us to learn exactly how God *forgives* sin, and how God *deals with* sin.

Suppose someone came up and punched you in the nose with their big fist. And suppose, in an act of compassion, you were to say to that person who punched you in the nose, "I forgive you."

But they said to you, "Oh, there's no need for you to forgive me. I've already forgiven myself."

And then, another person standing by said, "Oh, well neither one of you need to worry about it. I have forgiven both of you."

And you were the one who got punched in the nose! Friend, listen to me. Only the punch-*ee* can forgive the punch-*er*. Understand that sin is a clenched fist in the face of God, and only God can forgive sin. Away with all of the psycho-babble that says we need to forgive ourselves, that we need to affirm one another, and that we need to forgive one another. There is a holy God, and sin is an affront, a reproach, and a rebellion against that holy God, and that sin must be dealt with.

The Vicarious Suffering of the Cross

Our text points out three wonderful truths about how God forgives and deals with sin. The very first thing I want you to see is the vicarious suffering of the cross. The word *vicarious* means "in the place of another, substitutionary." Look at 1 Peter 3:18 again:

> For Christ also suffered once for sins, the just for the unjust, that He might bring us to God, being put to death in the flesh but made alive by the Spirit.

The just? That is Jesus—He who is just, and who never sinned; the virgin-born, sinless, spotless, stainless Son of God. The just died for the unjust. The unjust? That's me and you. He became our substitute. All through the Bible, God has been teaching the lesson of substitution.

The first day of Passover is also Palm Sunday. Do you think that is by happenstance? Oh, my friend, no. What is Passover? Back in the Old Testament, God wanted to give a prophecy and a picture of the cross of the Lord Jesus Christ. So He instituted the ritual of the Passover lamb.

There was judgment upon the land because of sin, but God told His people to take a lamb, a spotless lamb without blemish, and kill it. The blood of the lamb was to be shed and then they were to take the blood and put the blood of that lamb upon the doorposts of their house (Exodus 12:1-13). Not on the inside of the door, but on the outside. Openly, publicly, unashamedly, they were to paint the blood of the lamb on the doorposts.

Have you thought about this: it was to be upon the lintel and the side posts. Now think of a person with a hyssop branch dipped in blood—and he puts that blood up this side post, and across the lintel, and down the other side post. What has he done? Has he made the sign of the cross?

Even there, so long ago, God is picturing and prophesying that *it is the blood.* And God said to those Israelites so long ago, "When I see the blood, I will pass over you." That is how we get the word *Passover.* God will *pass over* you when the blood is applied. If you put the blood beneath your feet and you pass over the blood, God will not pass over you, but when you put yourself *under* the blood, then the death angel and the judgment of Almighty God will pass over you.

This Passover lamb is a picture of the Lord Jesus Christ. Let's back up to 1 Peter 1, beginning in verse 18:

> Knowing that you were not redeemed with corruptible things, like silver or gold, from your aimless conduct received by tradition from your fathers, but with the precious blood of Christ, as of a lamb without blemish and without spot. (vv. 18-19)

Jesus is the Passover Lamb. He is the lamb without blemish and without spot. Over here is the Mount of Olives where Jesus prayed in Gethsemane. Over here is Mount Moriah, where Jesus Christ will die. Mount Moriah is the same place where Abraham was willing to offer up his only begotten son, Isaac (Genesis 22:1-13). Mount Moriah is also the same place where the Temple was built.

And down here is Bethlehem, where Jesus was born, not many miles away. By the time of Christ, the priests and the Levites had instructed a special rank of shepherds to raise very special lambs: Passover lambs. These were the finest, the best, and they were raised in Bethlehem.

On Passover week, those lambs would be coming from the fields of Boaz in Bethlehem, up to the Temple Mount, Mount

Moriah. They would be going in through the Sheep Gate, up there to be examined by the high priests and the other priests and the Levites. And on the same day, coming down from the Mount of Olives, riding upon a donkey, is the Lord Jesus Christ—God's Lamb—going up to Mount Moriah.

On the same day, the Passover lambs and God's Lamb entered into the city. Palm Sunday, Passover—the same day, this day so long ago.

When those Passover lambs came, the priests began to look at them and examine them. They would look inside the mouth. They would go through the fleece, the little hooves, the eyes; even the eyelids were examined. If there was any flaw, that lamb was not worthy. He had to be a special lamb, a lamb without spot or blemish.

But at the same time those lambs were coming, God's Lamb was coming. You see, there was another Lamb born in Bethlehem. Mary had a little Lamb, and His fleece was white as snow. He never knew sin. He was the virgin-born Son of God, God's sinless Lamb, the lamb that Abraham talked about on Mount Moriah when he said, "My son, God will provide for Himself the lamb…" (Genesis 22:1-13).

God would not provide a lamb *for* Himself—He Himself would *be* the Lamb. See how it's all coming together?

Have you ever wondered why so much of the Gospels is given over to the last week of Jesus' life? Have you ever thought about that? But why is it the *last* week? Because this is the climax of it all, and it is there in that last week that Jesus is being examined. He is being examined by the Pharisees, by the Sadducees, by the Herodians, by the civil leaders; and they all have to say, "I find no fault in Him. Never a man spake like this man" (John 19:6; 7:43-46). Jesus, as God's perfect Lamb, could look all of them in the eye and say, "Which of you convicts Me of sin?" He was the sinless, spotless Lamb, and He was being examined.

Then came that day when the Passover lamb was to be slain. At 3:00 in the afternoon, the priest would tilt the head of that little spotless lamb, take his sharp, lethal knife, and slit the throat of the lamb.

At the same time that was happening, on cruel Golgotha, God's Lamb was pouring out His precious, ruby red, royal blood for the sin of mankind. Jesus said from that cross, "It is finished!" (John 19:30). It is paid in full. Priests, you can go home now. Levites, put away your knives! Shepherds, your job is done, because "It is finished." Amen? It is done. Hallelujah!

Jesus, God's Lamb, died upon that cross. The purpose of the cross is substitution. Passover has shown us this very clearly and very plainly.

When the Lord Jesus Christ died, He fulfilled yet another Old Testament symbolism. The high priest would take a goat called the scapegoat, and he would lay his hand upon the head of the goat and confess the sins of the people upon it. Then that goat would be led outside the city, and there the goat would be killed, and his blood shed.

That is the reason the Bible tells us Jesus died outside the city walls; Jesus was our scapegoat. Our sins were laid upon Him and He carried those sins to the cross; and in agony and blood, He died.

Here is another illustration. Pilate was there in his judgment hall, and he did not want to crucify the Lord Jesus. Pilate was a fence-straddling politician, and whatever buttered his bread determined his conduct. He was trying to get out of this situation, but the people were clamoring for the blood of Jesus. But Pilate thought he had an ingenious scheme. "Well," he says, "we've got another man here: Barabbas."

Now Barabbas was a thief, and a murderer. Barabbas was an insurrectionist, and Pilate thought, *Surely if there was ever a man that needed to be put to death, it is Barabbas.*

So here is what Pilate said. "According to tradition, we always release a prisoner to the people during the feast of Passover. We let them choose whom they will pardon. And so, we have here Barabbas…and we have here Jesus. Which of these two do you want me to release to you?" (see Matthew 27:15; Mark 15:6).

Do you know what the crowd said? "Barabbas!"

So Pilate said, "What then shall I do with Jesus, Who is called the Christ?"

The crowd said, "Let Him be crucified!" (see Mark 15:7-15).

This was the same fickle crowd that, when Jesus was coming in on Palm Sunday, were saying "Hail Him, hail Him!" Now they were saying, "Nail Him, nail Him!" Oh, the wickedness of human hearts! They were saying, "Let Jesus be crucified!"

And so they took Jesus, God's Passover Lamb, God's scapegoat, and they carried Him out. Jesus is the just for the unjust, and He is hung up on a cruel Roman cross to die.

But now I want you to picture another scene. I want you to see another Roman soldier, carrying a torch. He walks down a narrow corridor in a Roman prison and comes to a door with iron bars on it. He holds the torch up, and back in the shadows on a mat of straw is a man. That man is trembling like a bird caught in a trap. That man's face is the mirror of evil and yet fear is written all over him. The guard opens the door with his key and says, "Barabbas, get up and come with me."

Imagine Barabbas as he begins to plead, "No, wait! Wait, don't take me! Please, have mercy!"

But the Roman soldier says, "Barabbas, quit sniffling. I've never seen a man with the fortune and the luck you have. Barabbas, you rascal! You're not going to die, there's somebody else who's going to die in your place! Come here, Barabbas. Look over on that hill. Do you see the middle cross? Barabbas, that's the cross we've made for you. But there is someone else on that cross. He has taken your place."

I don't mean to infer that Barabbas was ever saved, but I am saying that God has arranged a perfect picture of substitution. "...the just for the unjust, that He might bring us to God..." (1 Peter 3:18).

Look again at our text, 1 Peter 3:18. It says, "For Christ also suffered once for sins..." Tongue cannot tell, throat cannot sing, hand cannot paint the tragedy that was called Calvary and the suffering of the Lord Jesus Christ. There was emotional suffering, just as "Then He said to them, 'My soul is exceeding sorrowful, even to death...'" (Matthew 26:38). Oh, the emotional agony! Luke 22:44 says, "And being in agony, He prayed more earnestly. Then His sweat became like great drops of blood falling down to the ground."

Some years ago, somebody handed me an article from the Journal of the American Medical Association (JAMA). And in that journal, physicians were talking about the suffering of the Lord Jesus Christ. And they tell about this bloody sweat. This is what the article said:

> *Although this is a very rare phenomenon, bloody sweat (hematidrosis or hemohidrosis) may occur in highly emotional states or in persons with bleeding disorders. As a result of hemorrhage into the sweat glands, the skin becomes fragile and tender.*

(On the Physical Death of Jesus Christ—William D. Edwards, MD; Wesley J. Gabel, MDiv; Floyd E. Hosmer, MS, AMI—JAMA March 21, 1986—Vol 255, No. 11)

This is what happened to the Lord Jesus. He was in such agony that the minute capillaries ruptured and broke down.

Not only was there the emotional suffering, but there was also the bodily suffering of the Lord Jesus. They scourged the Lord Jesus!

The Romans knew how to scourge. They would tie the hands of the victim and hoist him till he was on the balls of his feet. This is to increase the pain. The back would become stretched smooth as silk. The scourging instrument was a whip, with a sturdy handle and leather thongs. And on the ends of those leather thongs there would be little bits of bone, and metal, and glass, ingeniously tied.

There would be two Romans to perform the scourging, called *lictors*. As the body was stretched out, one of the lictors would start whipping at the nape of the neck and work downward. The other would start at the ankles and work upward. As a team, they would flay that person stretched out there, standing on the balls of his feet. The whip would reach around the body and each time as it was pulled back, it pulled away a piece of flesh. They knew how to pull away the flesh so as to expose the nerves and the muscles without disemboweling the individual.

After a man was cut loose from being scourged and fell to the ground, he did not walk away...he crawled away. That is the reason the Bible says they *took* Him to the judgment hall (see Matthew

27:27). He was too weak to walk. You can understand why, later, Jesus stumbled and fell beneath the cross. They battered Him with their fists. They beat Him with clubs. Then they took Him out for the actual crucifixion.

Do you know why the Romans used crucifixion? Do you know why they used the cross? You talk about cruel and unusual punishment!

Crucifixion was meant to be cruel, meant to be unusual. Crucifixion was meant to inspire stark terror. Anybody who saw a crucifixion said, "Whatever caused that, I will not do. Romans, whatever you tell me to do, I'll do it. But don't crucify me!"

Have you ever heard the word *excruciating*? That comes from the Latin word *excruciatos*, which literally means "out of the cross." Our word *excruciating* comes from crucifixion, from the cross's kind of pain.

The Romans would nail the victim's hand to the cross. They would separate the metacarpals and put the nail right between them. Not in the palm of the hand, but in the wrist, so that the body would not fall from the cross. They would try to hit the median nerve with the nail to send pain up the body and into the torso.

The crucified man would be nailed with his hands at a 90° angle from his head, but when the weight of the body would fall, the arms went up to a 65° angle. The feet were nailed to the cross. The weight of the body comes down on the chest and the person who is crucified is gasping for breath.

In order to breathe, he has to lift himself, but in order to lift himself, he has to push down on those nails in his feet and so he is between gasping for breath and searing with pain. There is nausea, and shock, and searing pain as every nerve in that body becomes a pathway for the feel of pain. The individual stays there an agonizingly long time and dies an *excruciating* death.

There was the physical agony of the cross and there was the emotional agony. Not only did Jesus Christ drink the cup that is the pollution of sin, but He also wore the crown that is the penalty of sin. The cup and the crown tell us of the cross and Jesus on it, with all that pollution, bearing the penalty. Not that He ever sinned; He was the just for the unjust. But He paid that price.

What was the price? Separation from Almighty God. Not only would God the Father be separated from Him, but He, for that moment, would become the object of the Father's loathing, and God the Father must look upon Jesus as God would look upon and deal with a sinner.

Now do you understand Peter's message? "For Christ also suffered once for sins, the just for the unjust, that He might bring us to God..." (1 Peter 3:18a). That's the vicarious suffering of the cross.

The Vital Satisfaction of the Cross

My heart was so moved as I studied for this message. Now I want you to see the vital satisfaction of the cross. There's a word in our text that I don't want you to miss. First Peter 3:18, "For Christ also suffered..." and what's that next word? *Once.* "For Christ also suffered once for sins..." That does not mean once upon a time. It means *once and for all.* This is a good place for an "Amen!" When Jesus said "It is finished" (see John 19:30), He meant the debt had been paid, absolutely.

In Rome, when a man would be judged as guilty for a crime, they would put that man in prison. They would write out a certificate of debt; that is, his debt to the State. His debt to society. And that was what his crime, his sin, had incurred. It was called a Certificate of Debt and it would be placed upon his prison door.

After he had done his time, paid the penalty, and satisfied the demands of the law, they would write across the Certificate of Debt that it was *paid in full,* and give it to him. Do you know what word they would write on it? *Tetelestai.* Do you know what that word means? *It is finished!* It is paid in full. That man wouldn't have to go back to prison again. He'd never come into double jeopardy. If they ever arrested him for that crime again and said, "This is what you've done," he could say, "Yes, but I have paid. It is done. You can't bring me in twice for the same crime."

This is what it says for us: Jesus has *once* suffered for sin, and what blasphemy it would be to say there needs to be another sacrifice for sin! Listen to Hebrews 10:12-14:

But this Man, after He had offered one sacrifice for sins forever, sat down at the right hand of God, from that time waiting till His enemies are made His footstool. For by one offering He has perfected forever those who are being sanctified.

Hallelujah! That's why I believe in eternal security. For if you were to ever get lost again after you were saved—which you never could do—but let's suppose you *could* get lost after you got saved. For you to be saved again, Jesus would have to die again.

You see, when Jesus died, it was good for one salvation only. "For by one offering He has perfected forever those who are being sanctified" (v. 14). Jesus said, "It's finished; it's done; it's paid in full." There's nothing you can do, nothing you need do. This is the vicarious suffering of the cross. This is the vital satisfaction of the cross.

The Bible says in Isaiah 53:11, "He shall see the labor of His soul, and be satisfied..." God is satisfied with what Jesus did on the cross. The sin-debt is paid.

The Victorious Salvation of the Cross

Here is the third thing I want you to see; not only the vicarious suffering of the cross, or the vital satisfaction of the cross, but also the victorious salvation of the cross. He hath suffered for sin, the just for the unjust, but why? 1 Peter 3:18 says, "...that He might bring us to God..."

What does sin do? Sin separates us from a holy God. What did the cross do? On that cross, Jesus took the holy God with one hand, and sinful man with the other hand, and "having made peace through the blood of His cross," He "has reconciled" God and man (see Colossians 1:20; 2 Corinthians 5:18). Look at Romans 5:10, "For if when we were enemies we were reconciled to God through the death of His Son, much more, having been reconciled, we shall be saved by His life."

All "that He might bring us to God..." (1 Peter 3:18). The word there for "bring," *prosago,* is a Greek word which can refer to taking an individual and presenting him to a king or a dignitary.

That's what Jesus has done—Jesus has taken us by the hand to present us to God the Father. He's saying, "Father, these are Mine. I purchased them with My blood on that cross." Does that excite you? It excites me!

King David of the Old Testament had a son whose name was Absalom, and Absalom rebelled against his father. And there was a woman in the kingdom who said to David, "You need to do something to reconcile with your son, and to bring him back" (see 2 Samuel 14). But David did not do it. So the woman said, "David, you're not acting like God acts." Here is what that woman said to David in 2 Samuel 14:14:

> For we will surely die and *become* like water spilled on the ground, which cannot be gathered up again. Yet God does not take away a life; but He devises means, so that His banished ones are not expelled from Him.

Isn't that a great gospel text in the Old Testament? We are like water spilt on the ground, and God does not show partiality toward certain people, and yet God has devised means so that His banished ones need not be expelled from him. God has a way of bringing us back.

I want to tell you a story—a true story. *Reader's Digest* recounted it, but I heard it from a preacher named Ravi Zacharias.

There was a man from New York who would ride the Long Island commuter train at 9:09 every morning. He was a photographer, and of Hungarian background. One day, he had a friend who was sick, and so this man—whose name was Marcel Sternberger—decided to stay with his friend over the morning, and go into the city later. So rather than riding the 9:09 commuter, he got on the commuter in mid-afternoon. He wasn't used to riding that train, and it was filled with people.

When Sternberger got on, a great host of people got off, but a great host of other people got on too, and Sternberger was looking for a seat. One man got up, so Sternberger plunged into that seat and sat down. Now, next to Sternberger was a man reading a newspaper—a Hungarian newspaper.

Sternberger, who could read Hungarian, looked over and sees that the man is reading the classified ads. Sternberger says to the man, just conversationally, "Are you looking for a job?"

The man said, "No, I am looking for my wife's name."

Sternberger said, "Well, tell me about it."

"Well," the man said, "during the war we lived in Debrecen, happily married. But the Nazis were there, and they began to oppress us. They came and took me away to Ukraine, to bury German dead. I was afraid to leave my wife, because I was afraid the Nazis would come and put her in a concentration camp. But I had to do it. I went, and when I came back home after the war, I couldn't find my wife. I asked around and they said, 'The Nazis came and took a number of people to Auschwitz; maybe your wife was taken there.' I began to read and study to find out what happened to the people who were taken to Auschwitz. Many of them, you know, ended up in the crematoriums, where they were seared and burned in the Holocaust. But I also read that when the Allies came, they went into that prison camp and freed some people. And I'm just thinking perhaps my wife might not have been killed. She might have been freed. And so I got to thinking, maybe the Allies took those people to America. And if they took them to America, where would be the point of entry? It would be New York. And I was thinking; if my wife would be in New York, she wouldn't know where *I* am. But I know my wife; she's a thinker. She would put an ad in the Hungarian newspaper. And so I'm just reading the newspaper in case, by chance, I might find my wife."

Marcel Sternberger remembered that a few days before this, he had been at a party where he had met a Hungarian woman. She had given him her name, and said that she had lived in Debrecen. And she had said that her husband was taken away to Ukraine.

Marcel Sternberger's mind began to run. He said to the man, "What is your wife's name?"

"Marya Paskin."

Sternberger, without saying a word, pulled out his wallet and got out a slip of paper. And on it was where he had written the name *Marya Paskin.*

Sternberger said, "Sir, this is very important—will you get off this train at the next stop with me?"

Sternberger didn't yet tell him why, but the man trusted him and they got off together. Sternberger even had Marya's telephone number. He went to a pay phone, put in a coin, dialed the number, and said, "Hello. Who is speaking?"

She said, "This is Marya."

Sternberger said, "I'm Marcel Sternberger. Do you remember me? We met at a party about three days ago."

"Yes, I remember you Marcel."

"Marya, do you have a husband?"

She said, "I don't know whether I have a husband or not. I *did* have one. But I've not seen him since the war."

"Marya, what is your husband's name? "

"My husband's name is Bela, Bela Paskin."

So Sternberger said, "Wait just a moment…sir, what is your first name?"

The man from the subway replied, "My name is Bela. Bela Paskin."

Sternberger said, "Sir, take this receiver. You are about to witness a miracle."

Bela Paskin picked up the phone and said, "Hello?…Marya! Marya! Marya!"

(Read the original telling, "It Happened on the Brooklyn Subway", *Reader's Digest*, May 1949.)

Reader's Digest told that story and then said: Skeptical persons will no doubt attribute the events of that memorable afternoon to mere chance. But was it chance that made Marcel Sternberger suddenly decide to visit his sick friend and hence take a subway line that he had never ridden before? Was it chance that caused the man sitting by the door of the car to rush out just as Sternberger came in? Was it chance that caused Bela Paskin to be sitting beside Sternberger, reading a Hungarian newspaper? Was it chance—or did God ride the Brooklyn subway that afternoon?

But I want to tell you friend: *there is a greater miracle than that.* God devised means so that His banished ones need not be separated from Him, and Jesus died on the cross for you. Oh the love that thought it—oh, the grace that brought it!

Chapter 7

THE CONQUEST

A teacher once gave an assignment to her students: they were to write an essay on the greatest living man. One student wrote an essay on Jesus Christ. The teacher said, "This is a wonderful essay, but you misunderstood. I said the greatest *living* man." The student rightly answered the teacher, "He *is* alive." Other men die, and stay dead. Jesus died, and then He rose again.

I was reading about Harry Houdini, the escape artist. This man was a genius; he could get out of anything. They said that he had the flexibility of an eel and the eyes of a cat. People tried all kinds of ways to keep Harry Houdini locked up.

Sometimes they would put him in a coffin and then bury the coffin, but he would get out. Sometimes, they would rivet him into boilers; he would escape. They sewed him up in canvas bags and threw him in the river. He would come out. They would seal him in metal milk cans and weld the top shut and yet, somehow, he would escape.

One time, they put him in a federal prison in Washington. Maximum security. He had been in there for less than half an hour when he walked out, and in the meanwhile he had moved most of the prisoners from one cell to another. He was an incredible individual! As his biographer said, he could escape from anything except your memory.

And yet, there came a day when Harry Houdini died—and friend, he did not escape. No trickery there. No skill, no flexibility there.

But there was another man who died—His name was Jesus—and He made the great escape. Jesus came out of His grave, and He arose. And now, I want us to think about some things that are true *because* He arose. There are five resurrection facts you're going to find in the fourth chapter of the book of Acts.

Begin with Acts 4:1-2:

> Now as they spoke to the people, the priests, the captain of the temple, and the Sadducees came upon them, being greatly disturbed that they taught the people and preached in Jesus the resurrection from the dead.

His Persecution Continues

The first fact is that His persecution continues. Did you know because Jesus Christ is alive, He is still being persecuted? Here we are in Acts 4 and these Sadducees are grieved that it is being preached that Jesus is alive from the dead. As you are going to find out, it was the apostles who were persecuted; but in the truest sense, it was the Lord Jesus who was being persecuted. The reason the apostles were being persecuted is that they had done a miracle. So look back to Acts 3:12:

> So when Peter saw it, he responded to the people: "Men of Israel, why do you marvel at this? Or why look so intently at us, as though by our own power or godliness we had made this man walk?"

Peter refuses to take credit for the miracle. Now look in Acts 4:10,

> Let it be known to you all, and to all the people of Israel, that by the name of Jesus Christ of Nazareth,

whom you crucified, whom God raised from the dead,
by Him this man stands here before you whole.

Do you get it? A miracle had been done, and the high muckety-mucks didn't like it. They thought they had been done with Jesus. The people were beginning to follow the Lord Jesus, and now here was a man who had been healed. Peter said, "Hey, we didn't do it. Jesus did it."

When the leaders were persecuting these apostles, who were they persecuting? Jesus! The apostles were just the hands and the feet of the Lord Jesus. He has a new body now; His new body is called the Church. He is still alive.

Do you remember when Saul was on the road to Damascus and Jesus appeared to him? "And he said, 'Who are You, Lord?' Then the Lord said, 'I am Jesus whom you are persecuting" (Acts 9:5a). Now, Saul might have said, "Well, whoever you are, I'm not persecuting *you*; I'm just persecuting these apostles, these Christians." But the point is so clear you can't miss it. When you persecute the Church, you are persecuting Jesus. Jesus is not dead; He is alive. You can't persecute a dead man.

Now this is an interesting thing. Why did they persecute Jesus? Why did they persecute these apostles? Why will they persecute you? Why don't they like us? Why doesn't the world love the Lord Jesus? You would think the world would be glad to hear a message like His, wouldn't you? You would think that people would love the Lord Jesus.

But they don't. Why?

Let me tell you something: the world loves the baby Jesus. Nobody has any difficulty with baby Jesus. They don't persecute Jesus because He was born of a virgin in Bethlehem, and they don't persecute Him because of His teachings. They don't persecute Jesus because He healed the sick and fed the multitudes. As a matter of fact, the world likes that message.

Come Christmas time, even the merchants who don't believe in Jesus love to play the Christmas carols in their store so they can sell more merchandise. They don't mind that. So which part of Jesus is it that the world doesn't like? The Jesus that came to destroy the works of the devil. *That* is the Jesus they persecute. The Jesus who is against rape, murder, greed, pride, abortion, sodomy, racial hatred, and all of these things. That is the Jesus the world cannot stand: the Jesus who said, "I am the way, the truth, and the life. No one comes to the Father except through Me" (John 14:6).

To put it down big, plain, and straight, when you stand for *this* Jesus, as these apostles did in Acts 4, this world is going to come down on you like a hammer, and all of the artillery of hell is going to be aimed at you just like it was aimed at the Lord Jesus Christ.

If you're not getting any persecution, don't boast about it. The Bible says "Yes, and all who desire to live godly in Christ Jesus will suffer persecution" (2 Timothy 3:12). Don't get the idea that the world has gotten more churchy if there's no persecution—it's only because the Church has gotten more worldly.

His Preaching Convinces

When you begin to let the living Christ live in you, you are going to find out that His preaching convinces. Look in Acts 4:4, "However, many of those who heard the word believed; and the number of the men came to be about five thousand." I'd like to preach when five thousand men get saved. Now, how was it that these apostles—fishermen, unlettered and uneducated—were able to stand up and preach and have five thousand come to Christ?

I'll tell you why: because He lives.

They were not dependent upon their power of oratory, their power of logic, or their winsomeness to bring these people to Christ. There was a living Christ inside of them! Anything I can talk you into, somebody else can talk you out of. I am not preaching facts about a dead Christ of history. I present a living Christ to you. I am not dependent upon talking you into believing in Jesus Christ.

If eleven of the disciple Thomas' friends could not convince him of the resurrection—eleven apostles who had seen Him with their own eyes—then *I* will not be able to convince you. Do you know what convinced Thomas? He had an encounter with the living Lord! And when he had an encounter with the living Christ, he was convinced (see John 20:24-29).

Do you know what you need today? An encounter with Jesus Christ. Not an encounter with the church, not with Adrian Rogers, not with choirs. You need to meet the living Christ. These people were brought in contact by the Holy Spirit with the living Christ and they were totally, absolutely convinced.

Other leaders come and go. They die. I visited Lenin's tomb once. I was in Moscow over the orthodox Easter, and I said to my wife, "We will not be in Moscow without visiting Lenin's tomb." The reason I wanted to visit Lenin's tomb was because I wanted to gloat a little, on that Easter morning. I wanted to go there and look at his dead carcass.

In the tomb, Lenin is there in a crystal sarcophagus, a crystal case. He is beautifully embalmed. There is his waxen face, with his beard trimmed just so. There's a soldier here, a soldier there, guarding Lenin. On that tomb, these words are written: "He was the greatest leader of all peoples, of all countries, of all times. He was the lord of the new humanity. He was the savior of the world." And yet, there lies that dead rascal. "He *was* the savior of the world"! Do you notice it's all in past tense? He *was*.

Jesus said, "I *am* He who lives, and was dead, and behold, I am alive forevermore. Amen. And I have the keys of Hades and of Death" (Revelation 1:18). Friend, I want to tell you: *that* makes a difference.

Where Lenin's tomb is, you're not supposed to whistle, talk, laugh, or even put your hands in your pockets. You're not supposed to say anything. My little wife is one of the greatest rule keepers in the world. But when Joyce walked past each of those guards, she just leaned in and whispered, "*Christos Voskrese.*" And that means, *Christ is risen!* He is risen indeed.

You see, it is an encounter with the living Christ that convinces people. That is the reason why I don't have to depend upon my ability to cause you to believe. My ability, my job, my joy, and my responsibility is just to bring you to that encounter with Jesus Christ. You see, because He lived, His persecution continues. Because He lives, His preaching convinces. *There* is the difference; we are preaching a *living* Christ.

His Power Confronts

There is a third thing I want you to see: not only does His persecution continue, and not only does His preaching convince, but His power confronts. Read Acts 4:5-11,

> And it came to pass, on the next day, that their rulers, elders, and scribes, as well as Annas the high priest, Caiaphas, John, and Alexander, and as many as were of the family of the high priest, were gathered together at Jerusalem. And when they had set them [the apostles] in the midst, they asked, "By what power or by what name have you done this?" Then Peter, filled with the Holy Spirit, said to them, "Rulers of the people and elders of Israel: If we this day are judged for a good deed done to a helpless man, by what means he has been made well, let it be known to you all, and to all the people of Israel, that by the name of Jesus Christ of Nazareth, whom you crucified, whom God raised from the dead, by Him this man stands here before you whole. This is the 'stone which was rejected by you builders, which has become the chief cornerstone.' (words in brackets added for clarity)

There was this man who had been healed; there was the power of the living Christ. They were confronted with it. Now, the religious leaders thought they were done with Jesus. They had put Him in that grave. They had set a seal upon it. They had said, "He is finished!" But *He* wasn't finished, *it* was finished: the plan of salvation.

The crowd had said, "If you're the Son of God, come down from the cross!" (see Mark 15:30). But that was the wrong challenge. They should have gone to the tomb and said, "If you're the Son of God, come out." He is shown to be the Son of God with power by the resurrection from the dead. And now, He is still alive, and He is on the loose. The rulers had thought, "We have finished with Him." But Peter said, "You crucified Him, but the same One you crucified has just healed this man!" They are confronted with the power of the living Christ.

And so are you in the world today. Skeptic, I want to tell you there are things happening in this world today that are being done by the hand of Jesus, and you can't deny it. I dare you to look at the evidence for what the Lord and Savior Jesus Christ is doing today! You think you're rid of Him.

Peter used a wonderful illustration they all knew: he talked about the cornerstone. Look again in Acts 4:11, "This is the 'stone which was rejected by you builders, which has become the chief cornerstone.'" Up there on Mount Moriah was where the cross was, and it was where the Temple was built; the cross on one side of Mount Moriah and the Temple built right on the top. There today sits the Dome of the Rock, but that is where Solomon once built his Temple.

Solomon, when he wanted the Temple built, said, "The Temple is to be built without the noise of a chisel." So they cut the stones for the Temple out of a great rock quarry *underneath* the Temple Mount.

If you ever go to Jerusalem, you can go into that quarry. I've been into it. You can go *way* back under the city of Jerusalem. And there, you can see where they chiseled out these massive stones for the Temple. They cut them exactly to shape, to the beautiful specifications that were written, and those stones were brought up to the Temple Mount to build Solomon's Temple.

Jewish tradition says that there was one stone, a very special stone, that was crated and sent up to the Temple Mount and left in the work yard. The workmen had to keep working around it. Sometimes they would stumble over it, and I suppose maybe bruise their shins on it. They didn't know what it was. So it got moved over to the side and finally it just fell over into the brook in the valley of Kidron, and bushes grew up around it.

But when time came for the cornerstone to be added to the Temple, the builders said to the people in the quarry, "Send up the cornerstone."

But the quarry men said, "What do you mean, 'Send the cornerstone'? We sent that a long time ago."

The builders said, "No, we don't have the cornerstone."

The quarry men just said, "Well, you better check again. We know we sent it."

You know where it was, don't you? The stone that the builders rejected became the head of the corner. They had to go down into the bushes, down in the valley to bring up that stone and set it there in its place. What was Peter doing on that day after the resurrection? He was saying, "Listen, folks. You thought you were done with Him. You thought you'd rolled Him off the Temple Mount and down into the valley. You thought He was in the bushes, in the tomb, but He is the One who is the head of the corner."

He lives! And because He lives, His persecution continues, His preaching convinces, and His power confronts. He is a living Christ and He is still doing miracles. I love this—after Peter says Jesus has become the head of the corner, he says in Acts 4:12, "Nor is there salvation in any other, for there is no other name under heaven given among men by which we must be saved."

That is one of the great, great verses in all of the Bible. Jesus is not a good way to heaven. Jesus is not the best way to heaven. Jesus is the *only* way to heaven. That is what it says, right there. If you don't like that, just go argue with the Lord and say, "Lord, You made a mistake in Your Bible." "Nor is there salvation in any other, for there is no other name under heaven given among men by which we must be saved."

Not the name of Buddha, not the name of Confucius, not the name of Allah, but the name of *Jesus*. Not the name of Abraham, not the name of Moses, not the name of any of the great Saints. There is one, wonderful name, and I love that name. His power confronts us today.

His Presence Compels

Here the fourth of these resurrection facts. Not only does His persecution continue, His preaching convince, and His power confront because He lives, but His presence compels. Read Acts 4:13, "Now when they saw the boldness of Peter and John, and perceived that they were uneducated and untrained men, they marveled. And they realized that they had been with Jesus." They had been in His presence.

Who is it we're talking about? Peter and John. Peter wasn't known for boldness a little while back. He had cringed before a little maid and said that he never even knew Jesus (see Matthew 26:69-75). Peter cursed, swore, and denied the Lord Jesus. But now, he had seen the risen Lord, and he was compelled. You could not shut him up!

You see, when you are in the presence of Jesus Christ, something happens to you. When you put an iron in the fire and leave it, before long that piece of iron gets red hot. Then not only is the iron in the fire, but the fire is in the iron. If you spend time with the Lord Jesus, you will be as bold as these people were. His presence will compel you.

What was it that set the rulers on their ear? What caused them to marvel? It was the boldness of these men for the Lord Jesus Christ. Do you know what we need in our church today? We need an epidemic of Holy Boldness. Do you know how we're going to get it? By spending time in the presence of Jesus.

What is holy boldness? Well, it's not arrogance. A lot of people think they're bold, but they're just arrogant. Holy boldness is humble boldness. Peter and John were not arrogant, but they were bold. Holy boldness is not self-confidence. You can have self-confidence, but that will turn people off. Holy boldness is not human courage, and it is not presumption.

Over in the hills of East Tennessee, some people—in order to show how "bold" they are—pick up rattlesnakes, and handle the snakes and kiss them and caress them. You can call that boldness if you want to; I call it tempting the Lord. I read one time about a man who was at one of these services, brother Steve Green. He was part of a quartet. He said he had gotten into one of these country churches, and didn't know what they were going to do. They began to handle snakes!

Steve Green asked his friend, "Is there a back door in this church?"

His friend said, "No, there isn't."

Steve Green said, "Well, where would you like one to be?"

What some people call boldness is not boldness. So what is holy boldness? Friend, it is knowing that Jesus is alive. I mean, listen: if you are truly, *truly* convinced Jesus Christ walked out of that grave, how could you ever be intimidated?

When the rulers saw the boldness of Peter and John, they marveled. They took notice of them. They were ignorant and unlearned men, but they said, "They have been with Jesus." We need an epidemic of holy boldness, to not be ashamed of the Lord Jesus Christ.

If you think about it, Peter and John were facing the equivalent of the Supreme Court. They're a couple of country bumpkins from Galilee, the hill country. They are fishermen. They should have been standing there just shuffling their feet with their heads down, afraid. But there they are, in front of the highest rulers of the land, in the magnificent Temple. They are absolutely uninhibited, with faces like the noonday sun.

They took a stand for the Lord Jesus Christ. They would not shut up, let up, or back up. They are preaching Jesus. I need some of that boldness in my own life, and you need it, too. I tell you, the way that you get it is to spend some time with the living Lord Jesus Christ. Friend, His presence compels us. We cannot be ashamed. We cannot back off.

His People Confess

Here is the fifth of the resurrection facts, right out of Acts 4. What happens when we know that He is alive? His persecution continues. His preaching convinces. His power confronts. His presence compels. And lastly, His people confess.

> And seeing the man who had been healed standing with them, they could say nothing against it. But when they [the religious leaders] had commanded them [the apostles] to go aside out of the council, they conferred among themselves, saying, "What shall we do to these men? For, indeed, that a notable miracle has been done through them is evident to all who dwell in Jerusalem, and we cannot deny it. But so that it spreads no further

among the people, let us severely threaten them that from now on they speak to no man in this name." So they called them and commanded them not to speak at all nor teach in the name of Jesus. But Peter and John answered and said to them, "Whether it is right in the sight of God to listen to you more than to God, you judge. For we cannot but speak the things which we have seen and heard. (vv. 14-20; words in brackets added for clarity)

Friend, the religious leaders said, "You can't preach a risen Lord. We don't want this message out." And why didn't they want this message out? Because of the power of the message! I'm told that one demon said to another demon, "If those liberal theologians ever really let Jesus out of this grave, hell help us, all heaven will break loose!"

That's true. The leaders knew that all heaven was about to break loose. You might as well have told the sun not to shine as tell these men that they could not preach a risen Christ. Because they had seen Him, you could not shut them up. Because He lives, His people confess. Anybody who has known that Christ is alive cannot keep quiet.

Some of you are not witnessing. Do you want me to tell you the reason you're not witnessing? It's right here in Acts 4:20. They said, "For we cannot but speak the things which we have seen and heard." A witness tells what he has seen and heard. Do you know why some of you don't witness? You haven't seen or heard anything.

A person who has seen and heard that Jesus Christ is alive cannot be made to shut up. If you are not telling people about Jesus Christ, to be frank, I don't think you understand that He is alive. I don't think you've seen anything. I don't think you've heard anything.

Here is the way the early church worked: "And daily in the temple, and in every house, they did not cease teaching and preaching Jesus as the Christ" (Acts 5:42).

They had been told, "You can't do it."

They said, "We are *going* to do it."

They were told, "We forbid you!"

The church said, "We're still going to do it."

Evangelism in the New Testament was not an eight-day meeting where they brought in some revivalists and evangelists. I'm not opposed to that. But in the New Testament, these Christians were all at it, and they were *always* at it. You know why? Because they had seen Him; they knew He was alive. You could not shut them up. His people confessed.

Think about what the early church did—they had no printing presses. They had no buses. They had no radio, no television, no loudspeaker system. They had no church building. And yet they turned the world upside down and inside out for Jesus Christ. They did so much, with so little. We do so little, with so much.

He is alive; His people confess it. Would you like to confess it? *He is risen. He is risen indeed!* Oh, let's get that in our hearts! Let's get that into our minds.

He is alive, and because He is alive, His persecution continues. And the way they're going to persecute Him is by persecuting you. Wear that persecution like a badge of honor, because *He is alive.*

His preaching convinces. Don't feel, when you teach or preach or witness, that it's up to you. All you do is bring them into an encounter with the living Christ. It is Jesus who convinces.

His power confronts. His power is real in the world today. Jesus Christ is still alive and well, and the Christ that walked the shores of Galilee is alive today through His new body, the Church.

His presence compels. Stay in the presence of Jesus. Just like you put iron in the fire and the fire gets into the iron, there will be a holy boldness about you. You will not be ashamed of the Lord Jesus Christ.

His people confess. They will say, "For we cannot but speak the things we have seen and heard" (Acts 4:20).

Let me tell you what New Testament Christianity is, friend. It is supernatural. It cannot be explained, and it cannot be denied. It will not be intimidated, and it must not be ignored. Christ lives.

Chapter 8

THE COMING

There is an old story which so well illustrates what I want to say: There was once a salesman who had been working very hard in the city. He had a hotel room, and he came in very late one night. He was tired and took off his shoes as he was sitting on the edge of the bed. He took off the first shoe and let it fall with a thud onto the floor. But he thought to himself, "That was so thoughtless of me. It's late at night. Dropping my shoe like that on the floor is bound to have disturbed the person in the room underneath me." So he took the second shoe and put it down very gently. He went to bed. In about thirty minutes, there was knock at the door. The salesman went to the door, and there was the man who lived in the room beneath him. The man had dark circles under his eyes, and he said, "Would you please drop the other shoe?"

The world is waiting for the dropping of the other shoe. The Christ who was born in Bethlehem—who walked the dusty shores of Galilee, who hung naked on a cross, who was buried, rose again, and has ascended the high hills of glory—that Jesus is coming again. The incarnation without the coronation would be like east without west. It would be like an engagement without a marriage. We are waiting for the Lord Jesus Christ to come. And friend, what a glorious time to be living, between those two mountain peaks of His incarnation and His coronation!

We are on a collision course with destiny, and we know that soon—and very soon—the King is coming. We cannot afford to be ignorant or indifferent as we wait for the soon-coming of our Lord. Now, we know that there are many people today who have hearts that are perplexed. Sorrow looks backward, worry looks around; but friend, faith looks upward. The King, the Lord Jesus Christ, is coming.

So let's look at our Scripture which describes the coming of the King. Here is what the Apostle John wrote about having seen,

> Now I saw heaven opened, and behold, a white horse. And He who sat on him was called Faithful and True, and in righteousness He judges and makes war. His eyes were like a flame of fire, and on His head were many crowns. He had a name written that no one knew except Himself. He was clothed with a robe dipped in blood, and His name is called The Word of God. And the armies in heaven, clothed in fine linen, white and clean, followed Him on white horses. Now out of His mouth goes a sharp sword, that with it He should strike the nations. And He Himself will rule them with a rod of iron. He Himself treads the winepress of the fierceness and wrath of Almighty God. (Revelation 19:11-15)

As we think about the coming of the King, I want us to learn three things from this wonderful, glorious passage of Scripture. How is the King coming?

Jesus Is Coming Visibly

There are those who always try to spiritualize the Second Coming of Jesus Christ as some event in history, or say that perhaps when a soul dies Jesus comes and carries the soul back to Heaven. Events happened in history. And indeed, we go to meet the Lord Jesus Christ when we die. But the apostles at the ascension heard the angels, "Who also said, 'Men of Galilee, why do you stand gazing up into heaven? This *same* Jesus, who was taken up from you into heaven, will so come in like manner as you saw Him go into heaven'" (Acts 1:11). Jesus went away literally, actually, bodily, visibly. Friend, He is coming back literally, actually, bodily, and visibly.

Notice what the Apostle John says in Revelation 19:11, "Now I saw heaven opened, and behold, a white horse. And He who sat on him *was* called Faithful and True, and in righteousness He judges and makes war." John says, "This is what I saw." You say, *"Well, John saw it; perhaps we won't see it."* But look in Revelation 1:7. "Behold, He is coming with clouds, and every eye will see Him, even they who pierced Him. And all the tribes of the earth will mourn because of Him. Even so, Amen." Now there are different cults and so forth who tell us that different events in history were the Second Coming of Jesus. Don't believe it. When He comes, every eye shall see Him; even the ones who pierced Him. That is, people of all times, even from two thousand years ago, will see Him. Jesus Christ is coming back visibly, in power and great glory and majesty.

Now that brings a question. "Pastor Rogers, what about the rapture? Doesn't the Bible teach that Jesus is coming like a thief in the night (see 1 Thessalonians 5:2; 2 Peter 3:10)? Doesn't the Bible teach that His coming is mysterious? But now we see this passage of Scripture that shows Him coming in power and great glory. Which is true? Is He coming in mystery, or is He coming in majesty?"

You must understand this or you are going to get hopelessly confused. There are two aspects to The Second Coming of Jesus Christ: first the rapture, then the revelation. The rapture is when Jesus Christ comes *for* His bride (the Christians). The revelation is when Jesus Christ comes *with* His bride.

Now I want to give you some ancillary Scriptures. In 2 Thessalonians 2:1, Paul says, "Now, brethren, concerning the coming of our Lord Jesus Christ and our gathering together to Him, we ask you," Christ is going to come and gather the church to Himself. We are going to be caught up to meet the Lord in the air. So Jesus is coming for His church first of all.

But then, in Revelation 19:14, we find Jesus coming *with* His church, "And the armies in heaven, clothed in fine linen, white and clean, followed Him on white horses." Who are these armies?

They are the Saints—that is, the Bride. We have just read about the Bride dressed in her wedding dress: white linen, representing the righteousness of the Saints. And so His coming is both a mystery and a majesty. He is coming at the rapture *for* His Bride. He is coming at the revelation *with* His Bride.

The Old Testament prophets didn't know anything about the rapture, so we don't find the rapture in the Old Testament. It was a mystery revealed in the New Testament. Paul said in 1 Corinthians 15:51-52,

> Behold, I tell you a mystery: We shall not all sleep, but we shall all be changed—in a moment, in the twinkling of an eye, at the last trumpet. For the trumpet will sound, and the dead will be raised incorruptible, and we shall be changed.

When the Bible uses the word *mystery*, it does not mean anything like a mystery novel. It means "a truth previously unknown, and now revealed." I understand that the twinkling of an eye is the fastest movement of the human body. Now that, friend, is a mystery that the Old Testament prophets did not understand. And it helps *us* to understand the various metaphors and illustrations used concerning the Second Coming of Jesus.

For example, in the Bible, Jesus' coming is described cataclysmically, like a bolt out of the blue. Matthew 24:27, "For as the lightning comes from the east and flashes to the west, so also will the coming of the Son of Man be." So Jesus is going to come suddenly, like lightning; but He is also coming secretly, like a thief. Look in 1 Thessalonians 5:2, "For you yourselves know perfectly that the day of the Lord so comes as a thief in the night." Well, is it a flash of lightning that everybody can see, or is it like a thief who comes quietly?

Jesus is coming sweetly as a bridegroom. Matthew 25:6 says, "And at midnight a cry was *heard:* 'Behold, the bridegroom is coming; go out to meet him!'"

But also Jesus is coming sovereignly as a king. Second Thessalonians 1:7-8 reads, "and to *give* you who are troubled rest with us when the Lord Jesus is revealed from heaven with His mighty angels, in flaming fire taking vengeance on those who do not know God, and on those who do not obey the gospel of our Lord Jesus Christ."

This passage would be antithetical and contradictory if we did not understand that there are two phases to the coming of our Lord Jesus Christ. First, He comes for His Church, and we are taken out before the Tribulation. And then, after the Tribulation, we come back *with* Him.

At the end of the Church Age comes the rapture, the Church being caught up. And after that in glory is the Judgment Seat of Christ, and the Marriage of the Lamb. The Great Tribulation will have been going on down here on earth. Then our Lord is going to come, and this is the point which we are talking about right now: when Jesus now comes with His church in power and great glory. What a day that is going to be!

That is the reason we are not waiting on any signs to be fulfilled. All of these things are going to happen, but we are not waiting on them. Jesus may come at any moment. If you don't understand that, you would have to think we're going to have to go through the Great Tribulation before Jesus comes. No, if you don't learn anything else from the book of Revelation, learn this, and get it down: Jesus may come at any moment.

I want you to hear what the greatest prophecy-preacher of all time had to say about the imminent coming of the Lord Jesus. By the way, do you know what His name is? It's Jesus. I want you to hear what Jesus had to say about His coming in Matthew 24:36, "But of that day and hour no one knows, not even the angels of heaven, but My Father only." Don't let anybody set a date for you. If anybody does, he is acting smarter than an angel. Matthew 24:38-39 continues, "For as in the days before the flood, they were eating and drinking, marrying and giving in marriage, until the day that Noah entered the ark, and did not know until the flood came and took them all away, so also will the coming of the Son of Man be." It is not the Great Tribulation that Jesus says we are to look for. Those people were eating, drinking, marrying, and giving in marriage; they knew nothing until that day. It was the ordinary round of life.

Matthew 24:42 states, "Watch therefore, for you do not know what hour your Lord is coming." And then in verse 44, it reads, "Therefore you also be ready, for the Son of Man is coming at an hour you do not expect." Mark 13:32-33 says, "But of that day and hour no one knows, not even the angels in heaven, nor the Son, but only the Father. Take heed, watch and pray; for you do not know when the time is." Jesus, in His humanity, had so divested Himself of that knowledge which was inherently His that He said, "Even I do not know; only the Father." The Church is not going to go through the Great Tribulation. If the Church was going to go through the Great Tribulation, when we saw the antichrist come and desecrate the Temple, we could just start counting. But the Bible teaches that we are going to be caught up before the Tribulation.

Jesus Christ is coming suddenly, at any moment. We are not waiting for the Tribulation; we're looking for Jesus. It is very important that you note what it says in 1 Thessalonians 5:9-11, "For God did not appoint us to wrath, but to obtain salvation through our Lord Jesus Christ, who died for us, that whether we wake or sleep, we should live together with Him. Therefore comfort each other and edify one another, just as you also are doing." The Tribulation is the great day of God's wrath. God will chastise His Church, but He does not pour *His wrath* on the Church. The wrath of God is for the unsaved. If I'm looking for the Great Tribulation, that is no comfort to me.

In Revelation 3:10, Christ is speaking to the church at Philadelphia, "Because you have kept My command to persevere, I also will keep you from the hour of trial which shall come upon the whole world, to test those who dwell on the earth." He said, "I am going to keep you from this terrible time." You say, *"Dr. Rogers, that was for the Church of Philadelphia two thousand years ago, one particular church."* But Revelation 3:13 says, "He who has an ear, let him hear what the Spirit says to the churches."

What Christ said to Philadelphia, He is saying to us. God took Lot out of Sodom before the fire and brimstone fell. God put Noah in the ark before the flood came. Those are times when God was pouring out His wrath upon the world, and God is not going to beat up His Bride with His wrath. He chastises us now, and "In the world your will have tribulation…" (John 16:33b). But the Great Tribulation will be poured out on this world after the Bride is taken out, after the rapture of the Church.

Jesus Is Coming Victoriously

The second thing I want you to see is Jesus is coming victoriously. Continue to read Revelation 19:11-13,

> Now I saw heaven opened, and behold, a white horse. And He who sat on him was called Faithful and True, and in righteousness He judges and makes war. His eyes were like a flame of fire, and on His head were many crowns. He had a name written that no one knew except Himself. He was clothed with a robe dipped in blood, and His name is called The Word of God. And he was clothed with a vesture dipped in blood: and his name is called The Word of God.

Now this one whom John beholds on a white horse—coming visibly—is Christ who is coming victoriously. All of this is a picture of victory.

First of all, see the mastery of His conquest. He is riding upon a white horse. When He entered into Jerusalem before Passover, the people were throwing palm branches in front of Him and bowing down and saying, "Hail Him, Hail Him!" (see Matthew 21:8-9). But in just a few days they were going to be saying, "Nail Him!" and they nailed Him to a cross. What was He riding into Jerusalem that day? A donkey; a lowly donkey. But when He comes the second time to Jerusalem, to the Mount, He will not be riding a lowly donkey. He'll be on a white charger. A white horse, in that day, was a symbol of victory, and honor, and conquest.

Secondly, there is the mystery of His character. Look at Revelation 19:11-12 again. The Bible says,

> Now I saw heaven opened, and behold, a white horse. And He who sat on him was called Faithful and True, and in righteousness He judges and makes war. His

eyes were like a flame of fire, and on His head were many crowns. He had a name written that no one knew except Himself.

That is the mystery of His character. He is righteous, true, and faithful. He makes righteous war. But the importance of this is that He has a name that no one knows. Did you know the Bible says, "Therefore God also has highly exalted Him and given Him the name which is above every name" (Philippians 2:9). What is that name? We know Him as Jesus. But there is a mystery about Him that you will never fathom, even in Heaven. He is the highest of the high. He is so far above us! One of these days, we will be like Him, but we will never be *as* Him. That was Satan's downfall; he said, "I'm going to be like the Most High" (see Isaiah 14:13). That is what he tried to say to Eve: "You will be like God" (see Genesis 3:5). No, Christ is higher than the high.

Thirdly, there is the majesty of His coronation. Christ has many crowns on His head. The word for those crowns is *diadem*. It is not a *stephanos*, meaning a victor's crown, but it is the regal crown that a king would wear. But Christ doesn't have just one; He has many, for He is KING OF KINGS. He is LORD OF LORDS, and no longer does He wear a crown made from the briars of this world, but a crown made from the jewels of Heaven. I'm going to love to see my Savior wearing that crown and to sing, "Crown Him with Many Crowns"!

Fourthly, look at the ministry of His crucifixion. Revelation 19:13 says that He has a vesture dipped in blood. Some people think this is the blood of His enemies. I think not—I think this is a reminder of Calvary. The Lord Jesus Christ forever wears an emblem of His sacrifice there. And thank God for the ministry of His crucifixion and the blood of Jesus Christ that gives the victory! We overcome by the blood of the Lamb (see Revelation 12:11), and the victory that He is about to win over the antichrist is based on the blood. What a day, when Jesus comes not only visibly, but victoriously.

What is the hope of this world? Is there hope? Yes, there is hope. But may I tell you that science is not the answer? Science has made the world a neighborhood, but not a brotherhood. As Dr.

Vance Havner used to say, "Civilization today reminds me of an ape with a blowtorch playing in a room full of dynamite." That is the situation we're in. Scientifically we're in graduate school; morally we're in kindergarten. Science is not the answer.

Politics is not the answer. No politician is going to be able to deliver us. We win the wars and lose the peace—and now these days, it seems like we can't even win the wars.

Social reform is not the answer. All that social reform does, if it prevails at all, is make the world a better place to go to hell from. It is not going to save this world. You know, sometimes people say, *"You preachers are pessimists, because you don't believe we can change the world."* I'm not a pessimist; I'm a glowing optimist, because I know the only One who *can* save the world! And I'm not in the business of rearranging the deck chairs on the Titanic. I am waiting for the Lord Jesus Christ to come again. Believe me, the answer to this world's problems, beyond a shadow of any doubt, is the coming of our Lord Jesus Christ. He is coming visibly, and He is coming victoriously.

Jesus Is Coming Vengefully

Thirdly and finally, Jesus is coming vengefully. People don't like the idea of vengeance. They don't like the idea of judgment. They think God is un-American if He judges sin. There are people who say, *"Well, you know God is too good to punish sin."* Listen to me: don't ever say God is too good to punish sin. God is too good *not* to punish sin. God is a Holy God. God has said, "'...Vengeance *is* Mine, I will repay,' says the Lord" (Romans 12:19b). Look in Revelation 19:14-16,

> And the armies in heaven, clothed in fine linen, white and clean, followed Him on white horses. Now out of His mouth goes a sharp sword, that with it He should strike the nations. And He Himself will rule them with a rod of iron. He Himself treads the winepress of the fierceness and wrath of Almighty God. And He has on *His* robe and on His thigh a name written: KING OF KINGS AND LORD OF LORDS.

This is Scripture: "the fierceness and wrath of Almighty God." *"Well, Dr. Rogers, I thought God was a God of love."* He is; infinite love, perfect love. But He is also a God of wrath. If you preach the love of God to the exclusion of the wrath of God, you don't have the whole Gospel. Now, each half of that truth is true, and when you take *part* of the truth and try to make it *all* of the truth, that part of the truth becomes an untruth.

God is a God of love. If you want to be saved, you can be saved. If you want mercy, you may have it. But I am telling you, as surely as my name is Adrian: if you refuse the Lord Jesus Christ as your personal Savior; if you trample under your feet the precious blood of the Lord Jesus Christ; if you spite the spirit of grace; if you turn from His longing hand that is reaching out to you and saying, "Come to Me, all *you* who labor and are heavy laden, and I will give you rest." (Matthew 11:28); if you ignore, spurn, refuse, or deny that, then you, my friend—listen, I don't say this with malice—you are going to face the wrath of God. God is a God of wrath.

Let me give you another Scripture that parallels this. Second Thessalonians 1:8 speaks of the coming of our Lord, "In flaming fire taking vengeance on those who do not know God, and on those who do not obey the gospel of our Lord Jesus Christ." He is coming vengefully to make things right. So many times, things are not made right in this world. Justice is not done. Wrong seems to prevail. Wrong is on the throne and truth is on the scaffold. It will not always be that way. Christ is the righteous Judge, and He will make it right.

So how is the King coming?

The King is coming back visibly. As surely as He was here the first time, Jesus Christ is literally, actually, visibly, and bodily coming back to this earth. Every eye shall see Him. You might say, *"Well I think we need to spiritualize it a little bit."* Did you know that there were those who missed the first coming of Jesus because they did not believe the prophecies? He is coming back visibly!

He is coming back victoriously. The kingdoms of this world will become the kingdoms of our LORD and His Christ. If you are saved, you are on the winning side. If you are not saved, you are following a loser.

He is coming vengefully. He is coming in flaming fire, taking vengeance on those who do not know God and who do not obey our Lord Jesus Christ.

What Does it Mean for Us Today?

Now what does that mean for you and me today?

We need to learn of His coming. You cannot afford to be ignorant of these things, and you need to teach others these things. The world needs to learn. Jesus said over and over, "Be ready, be ready, be ready."

We should look for His coming. We are not waiting on some prophecy to be fulfilled. If I thought that we were going through the Great Tribulation, if I thought the mark of the beast (Revelation 13) and all of these things were going to take place first, I wouldn't be looking for the Lord Jesus Christ. Rather than looking up, I would be looking around. I would not be waiting for someone to come; I would be waiting for something to happen. But we are to live every day as if Jesus were to come.

We are to long for His coming. The last prayer in the Bible is this, "...Even so, come, Lord Jesus" (Revelation 22:20b). We pray that model prayer, "Your kingdom come. Your will be done on earth as it is in heaven" (Matthew 6:10). Do you long for the appearing of the Lord Jesus Christ? I can hardly wait to see Jesus. What a day that will be!

But last of all, we need to live for His coming. Jesus said, "Do business till I come" (Luke 19:13). John Corts, of the Billy Graham Evangelistic Association, once told a story. He said that when he was a sixteen-year-old boy, he went with about eight of his cousins to their grandfather's farm; they were all out there having a big celebration. The kids wanted to go out and work in the field. But the grandfather said, "No, it's not a good idea. I don't want you kids out there." But they said, "Please, Papa, please. We want to go out and work in the fields." So the grandfather said, "All right. John, take them out there in the fields. You will not come in till the end of the day. Keep 'em out there for the full day."

They were so happy! They were on the tractor out there, pitching hay and all of that stuff. And for about an hour, it was wonderful. But then the sun came up, the hay was going down their collar, and they began to feel that grit and grime. So they said, "Aww, John, take us in."

But he said, "Nope. Papa said we're gonna stay out here all day."

"But it's hot!" They were hot, they were miserable, they were tired, they were whining, and some of them were crying and saying, "We want to go in!"

But John said, "No, we're gonna stay out here the whole day!"

And about three o'clock, there came an incredible thunderstorm, and the zagged lightning was going across the sky. The kids wanted to go in.

John said, "We're staying out here the whole day." Then, at the end of the day, about five o'clock, he said, "All right, we're going in." They got in the wagon and went in. They got their baths, had their supper, and got cleaned up. The kids were so proud that they had stayed in the field all day long. And then their grandfather gathered them at the supper table and said, "Children, I want to tell you something. God has blessed us. We have a fine farm here. We've got a good heritage. Let me tell you why God has blessed us: there have been times out there when it was hot and tired and grimy, and we wanted to come in. But we didn't come in; we stayed in the field. All this that you see is because we learned the lesson of work. We learned what it meant to stay in the field."

It has not been easy for the Church to stay in the field. It's not all honey and no bees. But I tell you, Jesus says that we are to do business till He comes. And when He comes, I want to be found faithfully serving Him. And I hope that you do too.

When He shall come with trumpet sound,
O may I then in Him be found,
Dressed in His righteousness alone,
Faultless to stand before the throne.

(From the hymn *"My Hope is Built on Nothing Less"*;
by Edward Mote, 1834)

CPSIA information can be obtained
at www.ICGtesting.com
Printed in the USA
BVHW040203290422
635494BV00005B/729